Dora's Decision

Katacha Díaz

Illustrated by Becky Radtke

Rigby.

Dora's throat was sore and scratchy again. At breakfast it had really hurt to swallow her eggs, so Mom had decided to take her to the doctor.

"Stick out your tongue and say *aahh*," said Dr. Aguilar, shining a flashlight into Dora's mouth. "You have a throat infection, and it's the fourth one you've had this year. We'll see how you do after you take the new medicine, but your tonsils may have to come out."

Dora wanted her throat to feel better, but she was afraid of having her tonsils taken out.

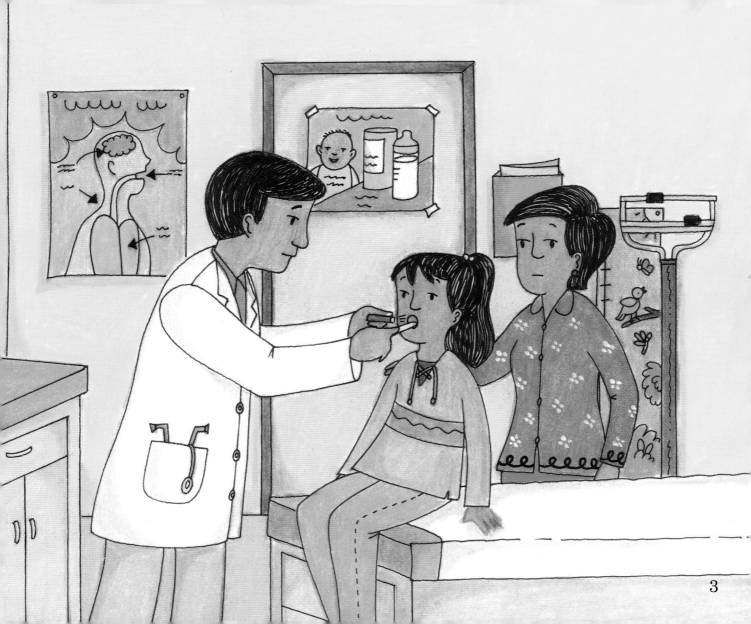

3

The new medicine had worked, but three weeks later when Dora woke up, her throat felt scratchy again. At breakfast she could barely swallow her toast. If Mom found out that Dora's throat was bothering her again, Mom would take her to see the doctor. Dora was scared, and she didn't want to have her tonsils taken out.

"I noticed that you didn't eat much at breakfast," Mom said to Dora later in the family room. "Are you feeling OK?"

"I'm fine, Mom," Dora told her. "I just wanted to finish reading my book."

"Are you sure that your throat isn't bothering you again?"

Dora nodded and went back to reading her book.

After she finished reading, Dora went to find Chico, the family dog. She asked Chico if he wanted to go for a walk.

When Chico heard the word *walk,* he barked and jumped up.

Woof!

As they were walking, Dora said, "I'm worried, Chico. If my throat keeps me from eating breakfast again tomorrow, Mom will know that I have a sore throat. Then she'll take me to see Dr. Aguilar. What should I do?"

"Woof," said Chico.

That night Dora's friend Daisy called.
"My throat hurts again," Dora told her.
"I've tried gargling with salt water when
Mom's not around, but it isn't working.
What am I going to do?" asked Dora.

"I don't want my tonsils taken out, and I'm going to be really upset if I can't go on our class field trip next week to see the play. Maybe if I go to bed early tonight and get plenty of sleep, I'll be okay in the morning," Dora added as she sighed.

"That sounds like a good plan," Daisy said.

Saturday morning Grandma and Grandpa got up early and went to the Farmer's Market at the park downtown, where they bought a large bag of oranges. After they got back, Mom and Grandma took turns squeezing the oranges to make juice for breakfast.

Farmer's
Market

"Why aren't you drinking your juice, Dora?" Mom asked.

"I'm not thirsty," Dora told her.

"Are you sure that your throat isn't bothering you?"

"I'm fine, Mom."

Dora loved orange juice, but when she took a sip, it burned her throat. She tried adding some sugar to make it sweeter, but she still couldn't drink it.

"I remember when your mom was your age," Grandpa said to Dora. "She kept getting throat infections."

12

"Dr. Rivera told us that your mom's tonsils had to come out," added Grandma. "The hospital was in the next town, and back then you had to stay in the hospital for three days! We went to see your mom every day, but we weren't allowed to stay the night. She was brave throughout the operation and her hospital stay, so when your mom came home, we surprised her with a gift. Grandpa and I bought her a gold charm bracelet!"

When Dora woke up the next morning, her throat hurt so much that she could hardly talk. She decided that she couldn't tolerate the pain anymore, so she finally told Mom about her sore throat. Mom was glad that Dora told her and said that they would go to the doctor's office the next morning.

At the office, Dora's throat was examined by Dr. Aguilar. He told her that her tonsils would have to come out. He gave Mom the name of a special doctor who would take out Dora's tonsils. They would go to see Dr. Robinson the next day, even though Dora's tonsils wouldn't be taken out until next week.

"The good news is that after your operation, you can eat all the ice cream that you want," Dr. Aguilar said. "The bad news is that your throat will be very sore for a few days, and you won't be able to talk a lot."

Saddened by the news about her operation, Dora called Daisy later that day.

"Guess what?" Dora asked Daisy. "I have to get my tonsils taken out next week. I'm really upset because I won't be able to talk for a while. Also, I really wanted to go to the play, but now I can't! I get to eat a lot of ice cream, but my throat will also be really sore."

"That is bad news," Daisy agreed, "but at least you get to eat lots of ice cream."

"Yeah, but I'd rather not have my throat hurt."

When Mom and Dad took Dora to see Dr. Robinson, the doctor explained that Dora would be asleep during the operation and wouldn't feel a thing.

"Kids usually have their tonsils taken out early in the morning and go home the same day," the doctor continued. "They rarely have to stay in the hospital overnight."

This was good news, but Dora was still afraid to have her tonsils taken out.

19

When Dora got home, Daisy came over and tried to make her feel better about going to the hospital. Grandma and Grandpa kept telling her not to worry.

"Are you scared about your operation?" Dad asked.

"Yes," Dora mumbled.

"It's okay for you to feel scared," said Mom. "I felt that way, too, when I had my tonsils taken out. Dad and I will be at the hospital while Dr. Robinson operates."

Mom, Dad, and Dora got up very early the morning of Dora's operation. Dora was hungry and thirsty, but Mom said that she couldn't eat or drink anything before her operation.

Dr. Robinson's nurse had explained that Dora would be wearing a special hospital nightgown, so she didn't have to take any pajamas with her.

22

It was also the day of Dora's class field trip to see the play. She was sad that she wouldn't get to go, but Daisy promised to tell her all about it.

Grandma and Grandpa
were up early, too.
"Don't worry," they
said. "Everything will be
fine, and you'll be back
home later today."

Dora, Mom, and Dad arrived at the hospital at 6:30 A.M. and went to the front desk. Mom and Dad had to fill out lots of papers. Then a nurse came over to ask Dora a few questions and to put a plastic bracelet around Dora's wrist that had her first and last name on it. The nurse asked Dora and her parents to follow her to a special room where they would wait.

The nurse came back a little while later and announced that it was time for Dora to change into her hospital gown. "It's not fancy," the nurse said smiling, "but you'll be comfortable during the operation."

Dora's hospital gown was pink. She liked the color, but it looked like someone forgot to sew it together! She would have to tell Daisy about this when she could talk again.

"Dr. Robinson will stop by to talk to you before your operation," the nurse said as she left the room.

There was a knock on the door, and Dr. Robinson came in and asked Dora if she was ready. She slowly nodded her head. Then the nurse came in carrying a tray with a small cup filled with medicine. She explained that the cherry-flavored medicine would make Dora feel sleepy, and she was right. After that Dora didn't feel nervous or scared anymore.

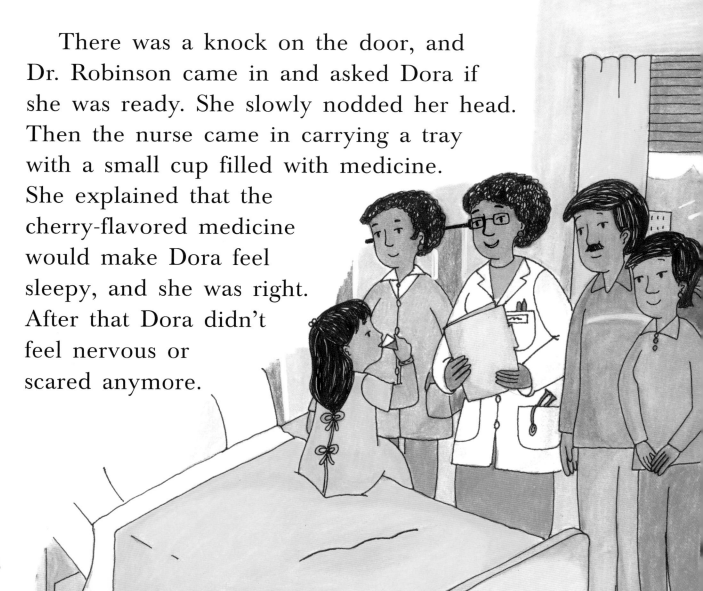

Two more nurses came in and moved
Dora onto a bed with wheels and took her
down the hall to the operating room.

"We'll wait right here, Dora," said Mom
and Dad as they each gave Dora a kiss. That
was all that she remembered!

When Dora woke up, her throat hurt every time she tried to swallow or talk.

"The doctor said that you did great, Dora," said Mom and Dad, "and we're very proud of you. Would you like some of your favorite ice cream?"

Dora nodded and smiled.

A nurse brought the ice cream and some medicine for Dora that would help take away the pain. She told Mom and Dad that Dora was doing fine and that she would be able to go home later that day.

When Dora got home she had some
more ice cream and then went to sleep.
The next day Grandma and Grandpa came
to see how she was doing and to give her
a present. It was a gold bracelet just like
the one they had given Mom years ago
when she had her tonsils taken out!

When Daisy came to see Dora after
school, she brought a videotape of
the play that Dora had missed.
It still hurt when Dora talked,
so she got a piece of paper
and a pencil and wrote
"THANK YOU SO MUCH!"

CHINESE COOKING

THE

HEALTHFUL WAY

CHINESE COOKING

THE
HEALTHFUL WAY

PAUL AND
JOANNE
HUSH

PRIMA PUBLISHING

PRIMA PUBLISHING and colophon are trademarks of Prima Communications, Inc.

Cover design by the Dunlavey Studio
Photographs © 1996 by Kent Lacin
Illustrations © 1996 by Camilla Stoltz

Library of Congress Cataloging-in-Publication Data
Hush, Joanne.
    Chinese Cooking the Healthful Way / Joanne and Paul Hush.
        p.   cm.
    Includes index.
    ISBN 0-7615-0297-1
    1. Cookery, Chinese. 2. Low-fat diets—Recipes. I. Hush, Paul. II. Title.
TX724.5.C5H868   1995
641.5951—dc20   95-33227
                                                                            CIP

96 97 98 99 00 AA 10 9 8 7 6 5 4 3 2 1
Printed in the United States of America

Nutritional Breakdowns
A per serving nutritional breakdown is provided for each recipe. If a range is given for an ingredient amount, the breakdown is based on the smaller number. If a range is given for servings, the breakdown is based on the larger number. Nutritional content may vary depending on the specific brands or types of ingredients used.

How to Order
Single copies may be ordered from Prima Publishing, P.O. Box 1260BK, Rocklin, CA 95677; telephone (916) 632-4400. Quantity discounts are also available. On your letterhead, include information concerning the intended use of the books and the number of books you wish to purchase.

CONTENTS

Acknowledgments

We gratefully thank our friends Ginger Shaffer and John Sarles for their computer skills and their invaluable help in preparing the manuscript for this book.

We are also indebted to Atlanta artist Camilla Stoltz for her very appealing pen-and-ink illustrations, drawn from her travels in China.

Our valued agent, Jeanne Fredericks, was able to find just the right publisher for the book, and our editor there, Alice Anderson, has been most pleasant and helpful all along the way.

INTRODUCTION

These days, many of us have new standards for the foods we eat. We want to cut back on fat, cholesterol, salt, and sugar. We avoid additives. We watch our calories. We know that good nutrition is part of good health. But being sensible is not all that matters. We have to like the foods we eat or we just won't eat them again. The real challenge in cooking is to make what *is* good taste good—and to have what tastes good be good for you.

Here is an answer: a way of Chinese cooking that is low in fat and low in sodium, yet highly flavorful. It is Chinese cooking that brings contemporary ideas and ingredients together with classic traditions.

How can there be anything new about Chinese cooking? A great strength of Chinese cuisine is its almost infinite variety. Traditional Chinese cooking techniques have proven themselves over many centuries, but many new flavors and food combinations are created as new generations of cooks try them out.

This is a book for our new generation. The techniques are Chinese, the ingredients are universal, and the focus is on healthful cooking. If you like Chinese food but have been concerned about high fat and sodium, then *Chinese Cooking the Healthful Way* is for you.

Many Westerners believe that Chinese cooking is too complicated and time consuming, and that many of the ingredients are exotic and hard to find. In our recipes we address these concerns. We use asparagus, broccoli, green beans, snow peas, cabbage, cauliflower, hot and sweet peppers, and standard cuts of meat and fish—all foods you probably are comfortable with. Special Chinese sauces and ingredients are called for too, but the ones we use are widely available, and we offer suggestions on where to find them.

We have taken special care to make the recipes in this book as clear, complete, and uncomplicated as possible. Remember that you don't have to commit yourself to a multi-course Chinese banquet every time you take out your wok. There's nothing wrong with making one Chinese recipe at a time and combining it with a simple salad, vegetable, or pasta dish to make an easy family meal.

This book shows you how to stir-fry and steam foods the Chinese way. It tells you about the sauces, marinades, herbs, and spices that are important in Chinese cooking. And the various styles of preparation and presentation that give Chinese food its distinctive look are also covered.

But it is the recipes that are the keystone to *Chinese Cooking the Healthful Way*. We include classic Chinese dishes as well as variations on them. Our versions are lower in fat and salt, but don't lack flavor. They are easy to like and easy to make. Perhaps best of all, they'll bring extra spice and variety to your cooking repertoire without adding too much in the way of calories.

CHINESE COOKING

THE

HEALTHFUL WAY

ONE

THE CHINESE STYLE

*W*hat exactly is a Chinese style of cooking? What makes it what it is? Partly, it is unexpected combinations of food—chicken and peanuts, sweet and sour, yin and yang. It is also the fast and fiery technique of stir-frying. It uses simple marinades and clever sauces. It is the look of diced and shredded ingredients, and special garnishes. It is tradition paired with innovation. It is imaginative, different, familiar, exotic, easy, surprising, comfortable, complex, and creative—all come together. And it can be fun, too.

THE WOK

Chinese cooking starts with the wok, the classic all-purpose cooking pan. With a wok, you can stir-fry, steam, slow-cook, smoke, and deep-fry (although we won't in this book) without ever having to put it in a dishwasher. The design of the wok is a classic case of form following function. It is as sophisticated as it is simple. The sides and bottom are rounded to spread heat evenly over its surface. (You can also buy a flat-bottomed wok, which is especially suited to an electric stove.) The sloping sides facilitate stirring with a cooking spoon and spatula. The top flares out to enable a bamboo steamer to be seated safely above the level of boiling water.

Most woks are made of carbon steel. However, because we seek the most healthful ways of Chinese cooking, we use and recommend a wok with a nonstick surface. The nonstick surface allows us to cut the fat in our recipes because we can drastically reduce the amount of cooking oil used. It may not be traditional, but it is smart. A normal carbon steel wok, like a cast-iron skillet, needs to be "seasoned" at home before use, by baking on a coat or two of cooking oil to prevent food from sticking. A nonstick wok goes this one better by having a still more effective nonstick surface put on at the factory. If you can't find a nonstick wok, you can use a large nonstick frying pan to achieve pretty much the same results. The frying pan isn't as aesthetically pleasing, or as well suited to stir-frying as the wok, but it will work.

The wok we use is a Danish-made, non-stick titanium wok sold under the brand name Scanpan. It is extra durable and holds up especially well to the high heat needed for stir-frying. And, when needed, it can be scoured clean with steel wool. We stir-fry with this wok using just a cooking spray. This enables us to eliminate the two to three tablespoons of cooking oil (usually peanut oil) that are standard in most Chinese stir-fry recipes. Three tablespoons of peanut oil would add approximately forty grams of fat to a recipe (seven grams of which is saturated fat). Eliminating this much fat is a major accomplishment.

The Scanpan wok is fairly expensive, but a number of other nonstick woks are on the market. They may not hold up as well, and you must never use an abrasive to clean them or the nonstick surface would be damaged. If you have a nonstick wok other than a Scanpan and are having trouble stir-frying using just cooking spray, add one to two teaspoons of canola oil instead of the spray. This will still achieve a major savings in fat.

STIR-FRYING
Now, with your nonstick wok at hand and an appreciation of how it will save on cooking oil, and thus fat, you're ready for some fast and fancy stir-frying.

The essential idea of stir-frying is to cook at high heat for a very short time—literally one minute or less for some ingredients, two minutes for others, sometimes three minutes for others—in order to cook the food evenly without losing its natural nutrients and color. For such quick cooking, the food has to be cut into small, uniform pieces so that every ingredient in the recipe is heated through and cooked just-so, but not overdone. This sounds tricky, and it certainly is a fast-moving process, but the recipes in this book give you specific preparation instructions and cooking times. Even if you're not an accomplished stir-fryer now, you'll quickly get the hang of it.

One thing to remember: stir-frying requires your full attention. Don't take any phone calls while stir-frying. Cooking at high temperatures takes careful preparation, proper timing, and continuous stirring and tossing of the ingredients to assure even cooking and to prevent food from sticking to the pan.

CHOPPING AND SUCH

You have to take time to save time. Quick-action stir-frying requires careful preparation. This means chopping, dicing, cubing, shredding, and the like—in other words, cleaver work. Here are a few suggestions. The best way to speed up the preparation work is to make it a communal effort. Try to get friends or family members to help you out. (Don't forget, though, to manage the process and instruct the neophytes.) Use a Chinese cleaver, a small Japanese cleaver, or a chef's knife. The knife should be good and sharp, as any good chef will tell you. Cut up the ingredients to just the size asked for in the recipe because the cooking times are related to those sizes. Trim off any obvious fat from meat. Put each chopped ingredient into a separate cup or bowl to be ready for its special moment in the cooking process.

There is no particular mystery about the various kinds of Chinese chops and slices. If the recipe calls for slicing, cut thin 1/8-inch slices (if it is meat, slice against the grain). If shredding is called for, cut 1/8-inch slices lengthwise into thin toothpick-like strips. If the ingredients are to be cut into cubes, the recipe will tell you what size. Diced pieces are very small cubes. Mincing is fine chopping.

STEAMING

Chinese cooking is not all stir-frying. Steaming food is also popular. This is a particularly good way to cook seafood, dim sum, and vegetables. Steaming retains the natural flavors, colors, and nutrients and keeps food moist and tender.

You may use a vegetable steamer or other steam cooker for the recipes in this book. Our preference, however, is to use a wok and a Chinese two- or three-piece bamboo steamer (this amounts to either one or two cooking racks plus a top). Just put three or four inches of water into the wok, bring the water to a boil, place the steamer into the wok with the food already arranged on the cooking racks, set your timer for the number of minutes called for in the recipe, put on the cover, and steam away.

It is best to have a 12-inch-diameter steamer with a typical 14-inch wok. Be careful that the steamer doesn't sit so far down in the wok that the boiling water reaches the lowest cooking rack. If it does, use less water in the wok. Otherwise, you will have boiled, rather than steamed, food.

An advantage of a three-piece bamboo steamer is that you can split foods between the two cooking racks, with fish and meats (that need more cooking) on the bottom level and vegetables (that need less cooking) on the top. Bamboo also helps absorb excess moisture. Use a heat-proof plate or line the cooking racks with lettuce leaves and place the food on top to prevent food from falling into the boiling water or from sticking to the bamboo. While steaming, watch to make sure the water in the wok doesn't boil away and burn your pan. Have a teapot with extra water boiling on another burner so you can easily add more hot water if needed.

DEEP-FRYING NOT SPOKEN HERE

A popular kind of cooking in most Chinese restaurants is deep-frying. This is simply frying food in a pool of very hot cooking oil, as is done to cook French fries. Deep-frying produces wonderfully tasty results that we all like—shrimp toast, egg rolls and spring rolls, fried won-tons and dumplings, and batter-dipped shrimp and chicken. But it also results in a high fat content, no matter how well it is done. If you deep-fry at home with less than professional skill, the fat grams can zoom right off the chart. So, to be consistent with the healthful way of Chinese cooking in this book, we are entirely forgoing the pleasures of deep-fried foods. We have been able to offer alternative recipes for some of these deep-fried favorites, and we can be comforted that there are plenty of wonderful, good-tasting, good-for-us Chinese foods that wouldn't touch deep fat with a 10-inch chopstick.

PRESENTATION

Part of what we enjoy about food is its appearance. An appealing presentation of food is a comfort to the eye and, perhaps, to the soul.

Chinese food lends itself to such musings. The complementary sizes of the ingredients in a stir-fried dish create a certain harmony. Contrasts in color and texture add interest and diversity. Garnishes are important decorative touches, and the little extra effort it takes to arrange food attractively on a serving dish or plate is time well spent.

Remember, as the Chinese do, that the food you serve is a reflection of you. The better it looks, the more pleasure it will bring to your guests and to you.

REGIONAL DIFFERENCES

Chinese cooking varies significantly by region. Foods from the western provinces of Szechuan and Hunan are spicier than those from elsewhere in China. Hot peppers, scallions, garlic, and ginger are used abundantly.

In the north, in Beijing and Shantung province, the seasonings are more subtle. You are more apt to find bread, noodles, dumplings, and buns among the staple foods, rather than rice. From the north comes mandarin cooking, the grand and elegant foods historically served at the banquets of the emperors.

From the south of China, in the region formerly called Canton in the English-speaking world, come many of the stir-fried treasures of Chinese cooking. Cantonese cooking is perhaps the best known of Chinese regional cuisines. Many of the early emigrants from China were from Canton, and the restaurants they started emphasized Cantonese foods.

In the pages that follow, we provide healthful renditions of dishes from the north, south, east, and west of China. Each region contributes in its special way to the appealing diversity of Chinese cooking.

TWO

A HEALTHFUL WAY

Most people who pick up this book believe, as we do, that what and how they eat is important to their health. Good sense and the preponderance of evidence tell us that good nutrition contributes to better health and a longer life. The American Heart Association, the American Cancer Society, and other medical and research groups tell us so too.

The question is, how do we bring better nutrition into our lives without too much pain and suffering? You can start by getting the American Heart Association's *Fat and Cholesterol Counter.* This book, and others like it, are available in libraries and all bookstores. It gives you an appreciation of what makes up a healthful eating program, allowing you to then set reasonable nutrition goals for your cooking.

The American Heart Association recommends that you determine daily fat, cholesterol, and sodium intake on the basis of your age, degree of activity, and ideal weight. For most people, this comes out to a daily budget of between 1,600 and 2,400 calories. Taking a mid-point of 2,000 calories (this is the average used on most food labels), the American Heart Association recommends that a daily diet include no more than 67 grams of fat and, of that, just 22 grams of saturated fat. Sodium should be restricted to 3,000 milligrams each day.

How easy it is to manage a nutrition budget like this depends on your motivation and will power. But when you read the *Fat and Cholesterol Counter* and then start looking at the nutrition information on food labels, you may be surprised at how quickly you become sensitized to nutrition considerations. You'll start to make adjustments in your buying and eating habits. You'll probably switch to skim or 1 percent milk. You'll try substitutes for butter and eggs. You'll look for lowfat foods, dressings, sauces, and desserts, and some of these will be good enough that you will stick with them. You will become aware of the huge amounts of fat contained in many fast foods, and you will cut back on those. You will also try to eat more fruits, vegetables, grains, and fish, and less red meat.

This doesn't mean giving up on all the foods you like. It does mean finding an improved nutritional balance that works for you. You might even lose some weight along the way. We each lost fifteen pounds in the process of doing this book—and that even takes into account the times we fell off the wagon to have a steak or hamburger or apple pie with ice cream. It seems to be all right to have a few nutritional lapses if you balance these out with sensible eating the rest of the time.

Now, how does this relate to Chinese food? Chinese cooking has always been one of the most healthful cuisines. It uses more vegetables and less meat than most other national cuisines. Its main cooking methods—stir-frying and steaming—retain the nutrients in food. But there has been one real problem. Many favorite Chinese foods are deep-fried in oil, which of course results in a very high fat content. And the amount of cooking oil used in most stir-fry recipes is itself enough to be a significant source of fat. Just the three tablespoons of cooking oil used in a traditional stir-fry recipe amounts to some 10 percent to 20 percent of the daily maximum fat suggested by the American Heart Association.

To make Chinese cooking really healthful then, we need first to cut out the use of cooking oil. That's what we have done by using a nonstick wok and lowfat cooking spray in place of cooking oil. We also have completely eliminated deep-frying because there is no way to get lowfat results from this type of cooking. We do offer, however, lower fat ways to cook some traditional deep-fried Chinese foods, such as spring rolls.

We use lean cuts of meat and poultry without the skin, and our recipes have less meat per serving than is usual in the traditional Chinese versions. In most meat-and-vegetable recipes, we cut the meat portion from four or more ounces per serving to two or three ounces per serving, with an offsetting increase in vegetables. This achieves a noticeable decrease in fat without an especially noticeable change in the look or taste of the food.

We also have made significant attempts to cut back on sodium. Soy sauce is high in sodium, so we use low-sodium soy sauce and call for less than usual amounts. Chicken broth, used in many Chinese sauces, is also very high in sodium if you use a canned version. We use either a "very low sodium" packaged broth that is available in supermarkets, or we make our own chicken or vegetable broth at home, with no salt added. We provide the recipes for low-sodium chicken and vegetable broths in chapter 5.

The wonderful thing about Chinese cuisine is that reducing the fat and sodium doesn't sacrifice taste. The herbs and spices, sauces and marinades, and cooking techniques that give Chinese food its special flavor still prevail.

To make it easy for you to fit our recipes into your nutritional planning, we provide a nutritional breakdown for each recipe that lists calories, fat, saturated fat, cholesterol, carbohydrate, protein, and sodium. The breakdowns were compiled using the computer nutrition program "Cooking/Diet for Windows" along with information from the American Heart Association's *Fat and Cholesterol Counter* and individual food labels.

THREE

A Simple Way

Some of you will be new to Chinese cooking. Others of you may have tried it and, perhaps, become bogged down in looking for hard-to-find ingredients or trying to do too many recipes at the same meal. Even an expert cook can find this to be intimidating.

We want to show you that Chinese cooking is not only sensible and healthful, it can also be easy. We have tried to select recipes practical for every kitchen. Once you get used to stir-frying and realize that 95 percent of the ingredients used in Chinese cooking are the same ones you use every day of the week, the intimidation factor disappears. There is no reason you shouldn't be as comfortable whipping up a Chinese entrée on any given Wednesday night as you are in doing an Italian pasta or your favorite Mexican creation.

Easy Menu Planning

It is traditional in Chinese restaurants to order and share several different entrées. Four people might select four separate dishes and each person would try some of each dish. At home, except for very special occasions, it is just not realistic for most of us to cook this way. It is simple enough, though, to cook a single Chinese entrée and serve it with rice or pasta, or a salad or vegetable side dish that might, or might not, be Chinese. You could choose a soup, salad, or vegetable recipe from this book, or just use your own favorite side dish.

If and when you are ready to put everything together into a Chinese banquet for six or eight of your closest friends, that's great. You can certainly do that too using the recipes in this book.

ABOUT THE RECIPES

At first glance, our recipes may look to be long and complicated. There is almost always a sauce to prepare and often a marinade. There is chopping and dicing to be done, and everything needs to be carefully organized. That's the nature of Chinese cooking. But the cooking itself usually takes only a few minutes.

We have enumerated the cooking steps because stir-frying should happen like clockwork; the procedures must be quick and easy to follow in a specific order. We have also used a system we call "On Your Tray" to remind you to have all the ingredients prepared and ready at your fingertips in separate bowls or cups, and placed on a tray or on your counter. If something is missing when you start to stir-fry, it is too late to scramble around for it. Once you get used to the organization of these recipes, we think you will find them easy to use.

All the ingredients we call for in these recipes are used in Chinese cooking, but a few of the fish varieties, the turkey, and some of the vegetables and fruits are not frequently found in classic Chinese recipes. In the interest of good nutrition and contemporary tastes, we have taken some liberties with tradition in the creation of these recipes, particularly with the salads and fish entrées. But we've tried to stay true to the spirit of Chinese cooking. We hope you enjoy *Chinese Cooking the Healthful Way*.

FOUR

APPETIZERS AND DIM SUM

Wok-Seared Sea Scallops

Chicken on Skewers with Spicy Peanut Sauce

Skewered Shrimp with Lime and Coriander

Crabmeat Dip

Baked Sesame Chicken Bites

Water Buffalo Wings

Eggplant Relish

Steamed Mushrooms Stuffed with Scallops

Barbecued Pork Strips

Miniature Barbecued Pork Buns

Fragrant Beef Buns

Shrimp Shao Mai

Spring Rolls

Spiced Nuts

Steamed Shrimp Rice Balls

Basic White Bread Dough

Quick Bread Dough

Steamed Bread Buns

■ Wok-Seared Sea Scallops

Makes 12 hors d'oeuvres, serving 3 to 4

This easy and appealing hot hors d'oeuvre is a perfect beginning for a small dinner party.

> 2 tablespoons fresh lemon juice
> 1/2 teaspoon minced fresh ginger
> 8 ounces sea scallops (about 12)
>   Canola oil spray
> 1/2 red bell pepper, seeds and ribs removed, cut into 12 (1-inch) squares

1. Combine the lemon juice and ginger in a bowl.
2. Add the scallops to the bowl and let them marinate for 20 minutes.
3. Heat a nonstick wok over high heat for 2 minutes.
4. Carefully spray the wok with the canola oil spray. (If you have a gas stove, turn off the burner before you spray the wok.) Place the scallops flat-side down on the bottom surface of the wok. (Do not crowd the scallops. If necessary, work in two batches.) Cover and sear for 30 seconds.
5. Remove the cover and turn the scallops over to the other flat side. Cover and sear for 30 seconds.
6. Remove the scallops from the wok. Stick a toothpick through each scallop and top with a red pepper square. Arrange on a serving platter and serve while hot.

■

Each serving provides:
89 Calories
1 g Fat
0.2 g Saturated Fat
29 mg Cholesterol
3 g Carbohydrate
13 g Protein
184 mg Sodium

■

CHICKEN ON SKEWERS WITH SPICY PEANUT SAUCE

Makes 24 skewers, serving 12

This is an easy and popular hot hors d'oeuvre.

2 skinless and boneless chicken breast halves (about
    6 ounces each), fat removed
1 tablespoon low-sodium soy sauce
1 tablespoon dry sherry
1 tablespoon honey
1 teaspoon minced fresh ginger
1 teaspoon minced fresh garlic
1 scallion, both white and green parts, finely chopped
24 (6-inch) bamboo skewers
    Canola oil spray
1/2 cup Spicy Peanut Sauce (see index)

1. Cut each chicken breast across the grain into slices
   1/8 inch thick. You should get about 12 slices per
   breast.
2. Combine the soy sauce, sherry, honey, ginger,
   garlic, and scallion in a bowl.
3. Add the chicken slices to the bowl and let marinate
   for 1 hour.
4. Preheat the oven to 450°.
5. Remove the chicken slices from the marinade.
   Thread 1 chicken slice on each skewer.
6. Spray a baking sheet with the canola oil spray.
   Arrange the chicken skewers on the baking sheet
   in one layer; do not overlap them.
7. Bake for 3 1/2 to 4 minutes.
8. Remove the chicken skewers from the baking sheet
   and arrange them attractively on a serving platter.
   Serve with the spicy peanut sauce.

> ■
> Two skewers provide:
> 106 Calories
> 4 g Fat
> 0.8 g Saturated Fat
> 32 mg Cholesterol
> 4 g Carbohydrate
> 13 g Protein
> 145 mg Sodium
> ■

■ SKEWERED SHRIMP WITH LIME AND CORIANDER

Makes about 16 skewers, serving 8

 1 tablespoon minced fresh garlic
 1 teaspoon minced fresh ginger
 1 tablespoon low-sodium soy sauce
 1 teaspoon sesame oil
 1/4 cup dry white wine
 1 pound jumbo shrimp (about 16), peeled and deveined
 16 to 20 (6-inch) bamboo skewers
    Juice of 1 lime
 2 tablespoons minced fresh coriander leaves for garnish

1. Combine the garlic, ginger, soy sauce, sesame oil, and white wine in a bowl.
2. Add the shrimp to the bowl and cover. Let the shrimp marinate for 1 hour in the refrigerator.
3. Remove the shrimp from the bowl, but reserve the marinade.
4. Thread 1 shrimp on each bamboo skewer.
5. Preheat the oven to broil.
6. Arrange the shrimp skewers on a rack on a baking sheet.
7. Broil the skewers 3 inches from the heat, about 3 minutes on each side. (Brush them with the reserved marinade before turning.)
8. Arrange the shrimp skewers attractively on a serving platter. Squeeze the lime juice over the skewers and sprinkle with the coriander.

■

Each serving provides:
63 Calories
1 g Fat
0.3 g Saturated Fat
83 mg Cholesterol
3 g Carbohydrate
13 g Protein
146 mg Sodium

■

■ CRABMEAT DIP

Makes 2 cups, serving 8 to 10

Coriander and oyster sauce give this crab dip a distinctive Chinese flavor. The chilies, ginger, and garlic add the spice.

1   cup cooked flaked crabmeat
2   tablespoons finely chopped red bell pepper
2   tablespoons finely chopped green bell pepper
2   tablespoons finely chopped water chestnuts
2   tablespoons chopped red onion
2   tablespoons chopped fresh coriander leaves
2   tablespoons chopped scallions
1   teaspoon minced fresh garlic
1   teaspoon minced fresh ginger
1   teaspoon minced fresh green chili pepper
1   teaspoon fresh lemon juice
2   tablespoons oyster sauce

1. Combine the crabmeat, red and green bell peppers, and water chestnuts in a bowl. Set aside.
2. Combine the remaining ingredients in a food processor or blender and process into a smooth paste.
3. Pour the sauce over the crabmeat mixture and toss. Chill until ready to serve. Serve with chips or crackers.

■

Each serving provides:
27 Calories
0.2 g Fat
0.1 g Saturated Fat
16 mg Cholesterol
3 g Carbohydrate
3 g Protein
55 mg Sodium

■

BAKED SESAME CHICKEN BITES

Makes about 24 chicken bites, serving 6 to 8

We've made a deep-fried version of this sesame chicken appetizer for years, and it has always been a favorite party hors d'oeuvre. Now in the age of fat-consciousness we use this baked version. It's much lower in fat and (almost) just as good.

^{1}/2 teaspoon minced fresh ginger
^{1}/2 teaspoon minced fresh garlic
1 teaspoon low-sodium soy sauce
1 teaspoon dry sherry
1 egg white, lightly beaten
1 skinless and boneless chicken breast (about 6 ounces), fat removed
Canola oil spray
^{1}/4 cup sesame seeds, lightly browned in a dry skillet over medium heat
1 cup Spicy Peanut Sauce (see index)

1. Combine the ginger, garlic, soy sauce, sherry, and egg white in a small bowl.
2. Add the chicken to the bowl and let marinate for 2 to 3 hours, or overnight.
3. Remove the chicken from the marinade, drain, and cut it across the grain into ^{1}/8-inch-thick slices. (You should get about 12 slices.) Place the chicken between sheets of parchment paper or aluminum foil. Using the side of a cleaver, pound them to flatten a little. Remove the paper and cut each slice of chicken into 2 pieces.
4. Preheat the oven to 375°.
5. Spray a baking sheet with the canola oil spray. Arrange the chicken pieces on the baking sheet.

6. Lightly sprinkle the chicken pieces with the sesame seeds.
7. Bake for 3 minutes, or until cooked through.
8. Remove chicken bites to a serving tray and serve with the spicy peanut sauce. Set out toothpicks so guests can spear a chicken bite and dip it into the sauce.

Each serving provides:
69 Calories
3 g Fat
0.6 g Saturated Fat
20 mg Cholesterol
2 g Carbohydrate
9 g Protein
39 mg Sodium

■ WATER BUFFALO WINGS

Makes 24 wings, serving 6 to 8

Of course Chinese-style chicken wing appetizers would have to be called Water Buffalo Wings. This is not exactly a recipe that goes back to the Ming Dynasty, but it certainly works in contemporary Chinese cooking.

24 chicken wings
2 tablespoons dry sherry
2 tablespoons rice vinegar
2 tablespoons honey
2 tablespoons low-sodium soy sauce
1 tablespoon sesame oil
2 teaspoons minced fresh garlic
2 teaspoons minced fresh ginger
1 teaspoon Chinese Mustard Sauce (see index)
2 teaspoons Tabasco
1 teaspoon cornstarch dissolved in 2 teaspoons
   cold water

1. Cut each chicken wing apart at the first joint, separating the drumstick from the rest of the wing. (Save the rest of the wings for chicken broth. See index.) Remove the skin from the drumstick parts of the wings.
2. Combine the sherry, rice vinegar, honey, soy sauce, sesame oil, garlic, ginger, Chinese mustard sauce, and Tabasco in a large bowl.
3. Add the chicken wings to the bowl, cover, and let marinate in the refrigerator overnight, turning the wings occasionally.
4. Drain the wings, but reserve the marinade.
5. Preheat the oven to 350°.

■
Each serving provides:
149 Calories
5 g Fat
1 g Saturated Fat
49 mg Cholesterol
6 g Carbohydrate
15 g Protein
215 mg Sodium
■

APPETIZERS AND DIM SUM

6. Place the wings on a rack on a baking sheet and bake for 40 minutes. Brush once or twice, using 1/4 cup of the reserved marinade.
7. When the wings are finished baking, bring the remaining marinade to a boil in a wok. Add the cornstarch mixture and stir until slightly thickened. Add the chicken wings and turn them in the sauce to coat. Cover and cook over medium heat for about 5 minutes. Arrange on a serving tray and serve while hot.

■ EGGPLANT RELISH

Makes 2 cups, serving 4 to 6

Because it is served at room temperature, this versatile eggplant concoction has lots of possibilities. Serve it as a cocktail-hour dip with crackers or chips, a vegetable side dish at dinner, or combined with fresh greens in a salad.

1 large eggplant (about 1 1/2 pounds), peeled and cut into 1/2-inch-thick rounds
2 teaspoons salt

On Your Tray

- Canola oil spray
- Bowl of seasonings
- Bowl of dressing
- Bowl of cooked eggplant

Seasonings

1 tablespoon minced fresh ginger
1 tablespoon minced fresh garlic
1 scallion, both white and green parts, minced

Dressing

2 teaspoons rice vinegar
1 tablespoon low-sodium soy sauce
1 teaspoon chili paste
1 tablespoon sesame paste

Garnish

1 tablespoon chopped fresh coriander leaves

Preparation

1. Spread the eggplant slices on paper towels and sprinkle with the salt. Set aside for 30 minutes. (This will remove the bitterness sometimes found in eggplant.) Rinse the salt off the eggplant slices, drain, and place in a bowl.
2. Combine the seasonings in a small bowl.
3. Combine the dressing ingredients in another small bowl.

4. Bring 2 quarts of water to a boil and add the eggplant slices. Cover and simmer for 10 to 12 minutes, or until the eggplant is tender. Drain and cool. Cut the eggplant slices into 1/2-inch-wide strips.
5. Assemble your cooking tray.

Cooking

1. Heat a nonstick wok over high heat for 2 minutes.
2. Carefully spray the wok with the canola oil spray. (If you have a gas stove, turn off the burner before you spray the wok.) Add the seasonings and stir-fry for 15 seconds.
3. Stir in the dressing and then the eggplant strips and toss to coat. Remove the eggplant mixture to a bowl and let cool. The relish may be made several hours or a day in advance to allow the flavors to blend. Refrigerate until ready to serve.
4. Garnish with the coriander before serving.

Each serving provides:
31 Calories
2 g Fat
0.3 g Saturated Fat
0 mg Cholesterol
4 g Carbohydrate
1 g Protein
208 mg Sodium

STEAMED MUSHROOMS STUFFED WITH SCALLOPS

Makes 24 stuffed mushroom caps, serving 8

24 fresh mushrooms, 1 1/2 to 2 inches in diameter
1/2 cup bay or sea scallops, coarsely chopped
 6 water chestnuts, chopped
 3 tablespoons chopped fresh coriander leaves
 1 egg white, lightly beaten
 1 teaspoon low-sodium soy sauce
1/2 teaspoon Tabasco
 2 teaspoons dry sherry
 1 teaspoon cornstarch
    Canola oil spray
 2 tablespoons oyster sauce
 2 teaspoons cornstarch dissolved in 1 tablespoon
       cold water
 2 tablespoons chopped fresh parsley for garnish

1. Gently brush the mushrooms clean. Remove and
   discard the stems.
2. Combine the scallops, water chestnuts, coriander,
   egg white, soy sauce, Tabasco, sherry, and 1 teaspoon cornstarch in a large bowl and mix well.
3. Spray a heatproof platter with canola oil spray.
   Arrange the mushroom caps on the platter.
4. Spoon about 1 1/2 to 2 teaspoons of the scallops
   mixture in each cap, forming a mound in the
   center.
5. Top each mushroom with 1/4 teaspoon of the oyster
   sauce.
6. Bring 3 to 4 inches of water to a boil in a wok.

Each serving provides:
58 Calories
0.3 g Fat
0 g Saturated Fat
15 mg Cholesterol
5 g Carbohydrate
8 g Protein
125 mg Sodium

7. Place the heatproof platter on the rack of a bamboo steamer. Cover and cook for 6 to 8 minutes.
8. When the platter is cool enough to handle, remove it from the steamer.
9. Make a sauce by straining the juices from the mushrooms into a small saucepan. Cook over medium-high heat and stir in the cornstarch mixture, a bit at a time, just until the sauce is thick and glossy.
10. Pour the mushroom sauce over the mushrooms and sprinkle them with the parsley. Serve.

■ BARBECUED PORK STRIPS

Makes 6 to 8 appetizer servings

Everybody likes the taste of Chinese barbecued spareribs. This lower-fat alternative works well as a party or pre-dinner hors d'oeuvre. Try serving the strips with Sweet Duck Sauce and Chinese Mustard Sauce (see index).

> 1 pound lean boneless pork loin
> 1/4 cup chopped onion
> 1 tablespoon minced fresh garlic
> 1 tablespoon minced fresh ginger
> 1 scallion, both white and green parts, chopped
> 1/2 teaspoon five-spice powder
> 1/2 teaspoon black pepper
> 1 tablespoon ketchup
> 2 tablespoons dry sherry
> 2 teaspoons low-sodium soy sauce
> 2 tablespoons Chinese barbecue sauce (see note)

1. Cut the pork into logs 1 1/2 inches square × 5 inches long.
2. Combine the remaining ingredients in a large bowl and mix well.
3. Add the pork strips to the bowl, cover, and let marinate in the refrigerator for at least 3 hours, or overnight.
4. Preheat the oven to 400°.
5. Place the pork strips on a rack in a roasting pan. Reserve the marinade for basting.
6. Pour 2 cups of water into the roasting pan to cover the bottom. Do not let the pork touch the water.
7. Roast the meat for 45 minutes, turning and basting often with the reserved marinade.

8. Remove the pork strips from the oven, slice in
½-inch pieces. Have guests spear the pieces with
toothpicks.

NOTE   The flavor of Chinese barbecue sauce (also
called Char Siu sauce) differs from western barbecue
sauce. Seasoned with Chinese herbs and spices, it is
made from soy beans, unlike the western tomato-
based sauces. You can find Chinese barbecue sauce in
the Asian foods section of most large supermarkets.

■

Each serving provides:
126 Calories
5 g Fat
2 g Saturated Fat
48 mg Cholesterol
3 g Carbohydrate
16 g Protein
126 mg Sodium

■

◾ MINIATURE BARBECUED PORK BUNS

Makes 36 small buns, serving 10 to 12

2 cups coarsely chopped Barbecued Pork Strips (see index)

1/4 cup Sweet Duck Sauce (see index)

1 teaspoon minced fresh ginger

1 teaspoon minced fresh garlic

3 scallions, both white and green parts, finely chopped

1/4 cup pine nuts, lightly browned in a dry skillet over medium heat

1 recipe Basic White Bread Dough (see index)

1 egg white lightly beaten with 2 tablespoons cold water

1 tablespoon sesame seeds, lightly browned in a dry skillet over medium heat for garnish

Spicy Soy Dipping Sauce or Sweet Duck Sauce (see index)

Assembly

1. Have ready 36 (3-inch) square pieces of waxed paper.
2. Combine the barbecued pork, 1/4 cup sweet duck sauce, ginger, garlic, scallions, and pine nuts in a large bowl and mix well. Set aside.
3. Divide the bread dough into 36 small pieces and roll into balls.
4. With a rolling pin or your fingers, flatten each ball into a circle about 2 1/2 to 3 inches in diameter.
5. Place a rounded teaspoon of the barbecued pork mixture in the center of each circle of dough. With your fingers, pull up the edges of the dough around the filling and twist the top closed. Turn

◾
Each serving provides:
268 Calories
6 g Fat
2 g Saturated Fat
32 mg Cholesterol
36 g Carbohydrate
17 g Protein
274 mg Sodium
◾

the buns over so the twisted side is down. Place each bun on a waxed paper square.

6. Brush the smooth tops of the buns with the egg white mixture and sprinkle with the sesame seeds.
7. Cover the buns with a tea towel and set aside in a warm place to allow them to rise. This should take about 20 to 30 minutes.

Cooking

1. Bring 3 to 4 inches water to a boil in the wok.
2. Arrange the buns on the racks of a bamboo steamer. Leave enough space between buns so they don't stick together while steaming (2 to 3 inches).
3. Cover the steamer, place it in the wok over boiling water and steam the buns for 12 to 15 minutes. (Check midway through the cooking time to be sure there is enough water in the wok. Replenish with boiling water if the level seems to be getting low.)
4. Serve warm with the spicy soy dipping sauce or sweet duck sauce.

■ Fragrant Beef Buns

Makes about 12 large buns, serving 6 to 8

1 cup finely chopped Fragrant Spiced Beef Roast
     (see index)
2 tablespoons hoisin sauce
6 water chestnuts, finely chopped
2 scallions, both white and green parts, finely chopped
1 teaspoon minced fresh ginger
1 teaspoon minced fresh garlic
1/2 recipe Basic White Bread Dough (see index)
1 egg white lightly beaten with 2 tablespoons cold water
1 tablespoon fennel seeds, lightly browned in a dry skil-
     let over medium heat for garnish
   Canola oil spray
   Sweet Duck Sauce or Spicy Soy Dipping Sauce
     (see index)

Assembly

1. Combine the beef, hoisin sauce, water chestnuts,
   scallions, ginger, and garlic in a bowl and mix well.
   Set aside.
2. Divide the bread dough into 12 equal pieces and
   roll each piece into a ball.
3. Flatten each ball with a rolling pin or your fingers
   to form a circle 3 to 4 inches in diameter.
4. Place a rounded tablespoon of filling in the center
   of each circle of dough. Pull up the edges of the
   dough around the filling and twist closed.
5. Brush the tops of the buns with the egg white mixture and sprinkle with the fennel seeds.

Cooking

1. Preheat the oven to 375°.
2. Carefully spray a baking sheet with canola oil. Arrange the buns on the sheet, leaving enough space for expansion when they bake (at least 3 inches).
3. Bake for 15 to 20 minutes, or until nicely browned.
4. Serve with the sweet duck sauce or spicy soy dipping sauce.

Each serving provides:
144 Calories
3 g Fat
1 g Saturated Fat
20 mg Cholesterol
20 g Carbohydrate
11 g Protein
146 mg Sodium

■ Shrimp Shao Mai

Makes 18 dumplings, serving 4 to 6

Shao mai are Chinese dumplings filled with meat, seafood, or vegetables. This shrimp and water chestnut combination is especially good for serving as a hot hors d'oeuvre. These can be made ahead and kept refrigerated or frozen. Just reheat them in the steamer or microwave when needed.

Filling

- 8 ounces shrimp, peeled, deveined, and finely chopped
- 2 tablespoons finely chopped water chestnuts
- 1 tablespoon finely chopped fresh coriander leaves
- 1 scallion, both white and green parts, finely chopped
- 2 tablespoons finely chopped celery
- 1 tablespoon finely chopped onion
- 1 teaspoon minced fresh ginger
- 1/2 teaspoon finely chopped fresh green chili pepper
- 1/4 cup cooked rice
- 1 egg white, lightly beaten
- 1/4 teaspoon salt
- 1/4 teaspoon white pepper

Additional Ingredients

- 18 round dumpling wrappers (see note)
  Lettuce leaves to line steamer
  Spicy Soy Dipping Sauce (see index)

■

Each serving provides:
51 Calories
0.7 g Fat
0.1 g Saturated Fat
58 mg Cholesterol
4 g Carbohydrate
9 g Protein
164 mg Sodium

■

1. Combine all the filling ingredients and mix well.
2. Using your fingers, lightly wet the surface of each dumpling wrapper with cold water. Place a table-spoon of the filling in the center. Pull up the sides of the wrapper around the filling, pleating the edges to form an open-topped pouch.
3. Bring 3 to 4 inches of water to a boil in a wok.
4. Line the racks of a bamboo steamer with lettuce leaves to prevent the dumplings from sticking.

5. Arrange the dumplings on the steamer racks, making sure they are not touching.
6. Cover the steamer and place it in the wok over the boiling water.
7. Steam over high heat for 10 minutes.
8. Remove the dumplings from the steamer and place them on a heated serving platter. Serve with the spicy soy dipping sauce.

NOTE   Dumpling wrappers are available at Asian markets and some large supermarkets.

■ Spring Rolls

Makes 10 to 12 rolls, serving 8 to 10

Spring rolls, like egg rolls, traditionally are deep-fried. But here we offer a lowfat version. The spring rolls are first sautéed to brown them and then are heated through in the oven. We also use lower fat ground turkey instead of pork in the filling.

On Your Tray

- Canola oil spray
- Bowl of marinated turkey
- Bowl of ginger
- Bowl of cabbage
- Bowl of celery
- Bowl of carrots
- Bowl of bean sprouts
- Bowl of dressing
- Bowl of scallions

Marinade

- 1 egg white, lightly beaten
- 1 teaspoon minced fresh ginger
- 1 teaspoon minced fresh garlic
- 1 tablespoon finely chopped scallion, both white and green parts
- 1 tablespoon low-sodium soy sauce
- 1 teaspoon dry sherry

Turkey and Vegetables

- 8 ounces lean ground turkey
- 1 tablespoon minced fresh ginger
- 2 cups coarsely chopped green cabbage
- 2 stalks celery, cut on the diagonal into 1/8-inch slices
- 1 cup coarsely grated carrots
- 2 cups fresh bean sprouts, rinsed and drained
- 4 scallions, both white and green parts, chopped

Dressing

- 1 tablespoon low-sodium soy sauce
- 3 tablespoons rice vinegar
- 2 tablespoons hoisin sauce

Additional Ingredients

  Canola oil spray
- 10 to 12 ready-made Chinese spring roll wrappers
- 2 egg whites, lightly beaten
- 3 to 4 tablespoons canola oil
  Sweet Duck Sauce (see index)

Preparing the Filling

1. Combine the marinade ingredients in a bowl and mix well.
2. Add the turkey to the bowl and set aside for 20 to 30 minutes.
3. Place the ginger and each vegetable in a separate bowl.
4. Combine the dressing ingredients in a small bowl and mix well.
5. Assemble your cooking tray.

Cooking the Filling

1. Heat a nonstick wok over high heat for 2 minutes.
2. Carefully spray the wok with the canola oil spray. (If you have a gas stove, turn off the burner before you spray the wok.)
3. Add the turkey with the marinade to the wok and stir-fry for 1 minute. Remove the turkey and juices to a bowl and set aside.
4. Rinse out the wok, then reheat it for 30 seconds. Respray the wok with canola oil spray. Add the ginger and stir-fry for 15 seconds.
5. Add the cabbage and stir-fry for 3 minutes.
6. Add the celery and stir-fry for 1 minute.
7. Add the carrots and stir-fry for 1 more minute.
8. Add the bean sprouts and stir-fry for 30 seconds.
9. Return the turkey to the wok and stir to mix well.
10. Add the dressing and stir well.
11. Add the scallions and stir.
12. Remove the turkey mixture from the wok and set aside until it is cool enough to handle.

(continues)

Assembly

1. Carefully separate the spring roll wrappers. Lightly cover the wrappers with a tea towel so they don't dry out.
2. Working one at a time, place a wrapper on your work surface and spoon 1/3 cup of the turkey mixture in the center of the wrapper. Using a pastry brush, brush the outer edges of the wrapper with some of the beaten egg white.
3. Fold the wrapper from the bottom to cover the filling. Fold the two sides in toward the center and continue rolling until you have a cylinder. The beaten egg white will seal the edges. Place the completed spring roll, seam-side down, on a platter. Lightly cover with a tea towel while preparing the rest of the spring rolls.

Cooking the Spring Rolls

1. Heat a nonstick skillet over medium-high heat.
2. Cover the bottom with 1 tablespoon of the canola oil (not the spray).
3. Brown the spring rolls, 2 at a time, turning to cook all sides. Set browned rolls aside while you brown the rest, using additional oil if necessary.
4. Preheat the oven to 375°.
5. Place the spring rolls on a rack on a baking sheet and bake for 12 minutes. (You can also freeze the spring rolls after browning. Bake frozen rolls at 375° for 20 minutes.)
6. Serve with the sweet duck sauce.

■

Each serving provides:
182 Calories
5 g Fat
0.6 g Saturated Fat
19 mg Cholesterol
5 g Carbohydrate
9 g Protein
266 mg Sodium

■

■ SPICED NUTS

Makes about 3 1/2 cups, serving 16

This tasty snack is, alas, not fat-free because all nuts are high in fat. But we use almonds, which have much less saturated fat than cashews or peanuts. We also don't add salt, so this appetizer rates well on the sodium scale.

2 tablespoons salt-free seasoning, for example Mrs. Dash
2 teaspoons curry powder
1 teaspoon ground ginger
1 teaspoon garlic powder
1 pound blanched whole almonds
1 egg white, lightly beaten with 2 tablespoons cold water
   Canola oil spray

1. Preheat the oven to 225°.
2. Combine the salt-free seasoning, curry powder, ginger, and garlic powder in a small bowl.
3. Combine the almonds with the egg white mixture in a large bowl. Add the seasoning mixture and toss to coat all the almonds.
4. Spray a baking sheet with the canola oil spray. Spread the almonds on the baking sheet and bake for 50 to 60 minutes, stirring every 15 minutes.
5. Store in an airtight container. Serve as a snack or with cocktails.

■

Each serving provides:
193 Calories
15 g Fat
2 g Saturated Fat
0 mg Cholesterol
7 g Carbohydrate
6 g Protein
10 mg Sodium

■

STEAMED SHRIMP RICE BALLS

Makes 24 rice balls, serving 8

Why not start off your next dinner party with some Chinese dim sum? These shrimp ball hors d'oeuvres can be made ahead and then reheated in the steamer or microwave before serving.

Shrimp Mixture

8 ounces shrimp, peeled and deveined

1/4 cup dried Chinese mushrooms, soaked in hot water for 30 minutes

1 cup Chinese-Style Boiled Rice (see index)

2 tablespoons finely chopped water chestnuts

2 tablespoons finely chopped scallions

2 tablespoons finely chopped celery

2 teaspoons minced fresh ginger

1 teaspoon finely chopped fresh green chili pepper

1 teaspoon minced orange peel

1 egg white, lightly beaten

2 teaspoons cornstarch dissolved in 2 teaspoons cold water

1/4 teaspoon salt

1/4 teaspoon white pepper

Additional Ingredients

1/2 cup sesame seeds, lightly browned in a dry skillet over medium heat

Lettuce leaves to line steamer

Spicy Soy Dipping Sauce (see index)

1. Finely chop the shrimp into a paste using a cleaver or a food processor fitted with a steel blade.
2. Remove the mushrooms from their soaking water and drain. Remove the stems and discard. Finely chop the caps.
3. Combine the shrimp paste, chopped mushroom, and the remaining shrimp mixture ingredients in a bowl and mix well.
4. Using wet hands to prevent the mixture from sticking, form the shrimp mixture into 24 small balls. Roll the balls in the sesame seeds.
5. Bring 3 to 4 inches of water to a boil in a wok.
6. Line the racks of a bamboo steamer with lettuce leaves to prevent the shrimp balls from sticking.
7. Arrange the shrimp balls on the steamer racks, making sure none are touching.
8. Cover the steamer tightly and place in the wok over the boiling water.
9. Steam over high heat for 8 minutes.
10. Remove from the heat. Spear each rice ball with a toothpick and serve with the spicy soy dipping sauce.

Each serving provides:
113 Calories
6 g Fat
0.9 g Saturated Fat
43 mg Cholesterol
9 g Carbohydrate
9 g Protein
123 mg Sodium

APPETIZERS AND DIM SUM

BASIC WHITE BREAD DOUGH

Makes 1 loaf (30 slices)

1 package active dry yeast
1/2 teaspoon sugar
1 1/4 to 1 1/2 cups warm water (100°)
4 cups white bread flour
1 teaspoon salt

1. Combine the yeast and sugar in a small dish and add 1/4 cup of the warm water. Set aside until the yeast begins to bubble or froth, 5 minutes or less.
2. Place the flour and salt in the bowl of an electric mixer or food processor and mix on low speed. (Alternatively, you can mix the dough by hand.)
3. Add the yeast mixture and then slowly pour in 1 cup of the warm water.
4. Mix until the dough comes together in a ball. (If it seems dry, add a little more water.)
5. Continue to knead either by machine or by hand on a lightly floured surface until the dough is smooth and elastic.
6. Place the dough in a large bowl. Cover with plastic wrap and keep in a warm spot until the dough has doubled in volume. This will take 2 to 3 hours.
7. Punch the dough down with your fist. Cover with plastic wrap and let it double a second time. This will take about 1 hour. It is now ready to be used in a recipe.

■

Each slice provides:
62 Calories
0.2 g Fat
0 g Saturated Fat
0 mg Cholesterol
13 g Carbohydrate
2 g Protein
74 mg Sodium

■

■ QUICK BREAD DOUGH

Makes 18 (1-ounce) rolls, serving 9

If you are a bread baker, by all means, use your favorite white yeast dough recipe or the preceding Basic White Bread Dough recipe for the buns and rolls in this book. If not, this simple, quick alternative works well too. It tastes best, however, eaten right after steaming or baking.

    3 cups all-purpose flour
    1 tablespoon low-sodium baking powder
    2 teaspoons sugar
    1 tablespoon canola oil
    3/4 cup warm water (100°)

1. Combine the flour and baking powder in a large bowl.
2. Combine the sugar, canola oil, and warm water in a small bowl and stir well until sugar is dissolved.
3. Add the water mixture to the flour mixture and stir until the dough forms a ball. (This is easily done in a food processor or electric mixer.) If the dough seems dry, add a little more water.
4. Turn the dough out onto a lightly floured surface and knead until smooth and elastic.
5. Place the dough in a clean bowl and cover with a cloth to rest for 15 minutes. It is now ready to be used in a recipe.

■

Each serving provides:
158 Calories
2 g Fat
0.2 g Saturated Fat
0 mg Cholesterol
30 g Carbohydrate
4 g Protein
44 mg Sodium

■

■ Steamed Bread Buns

Makes 24 buns

Serve these rolls as a bread accompaniment with your dinner or use them to make sandwiches with Shanghai-Style Braised Turkey Breast or Fragrant Spiced Beef Roast (see index).

1 recipe Basic White Bread Dough (see index)
3 teaspoons sesame oil

1. Divide the dough into 24 pieces and form into small balls.
2. Using a rolling pin or your fingers, shape each ball into a 2 × 4-inch rectangle.
3. Lightly brush the surface of each rectangle with some of the sesame oil. Fold each rectangle in half to form a 2 × 2-inch bun.
4. Lightly cover the rolls with a tea towel and set them aside in a warm place to rise. This should take about 30 minutes.
5. Have ready 24 pieces of waxed paper cut into 3-inch squares.
6. Bring 3 to 4 inches of water to a boil in a wok.
7. Place each roll on a waxed paper square and arrange them on the layers of a bamboo steamer. Take care to leave enough space (2 to 3 inches) between the rolls so they don't stick together while steaming.

■
Each bun provides:
93 Calories
2 g Fat
0.3 g Saturated Fat
0 mg Cholesterol
16 g Carbohydrate
2 g Protein
92 mg Sodium
■

8. Place the cover on the steamer and place it in the wok over boiling water. Cover and steam for 10 to 12 minutes. Check midway through the cooking time to be sure enough water is in the wok. (Replenish with boiling water if the level seems to be getting low.)

NOTE   If you want to make this recipe really simple, substitute two packages of refrigerated biscuits for the Basic White Bread Dough and skip to step 5.

FIVE

SOUPS AND SALADS

HOT AND SOUR SOUP

LOBSTER AND SPINACH SOUP

CREAMY CORN AND CHICKEN CHOWDER

CHINESE CLAM CHOWDER

WONTON SOUP

CURRIED BUTTERNUT SQUASH SOUP WITH SHRIMP AND CORIANDER

HOT PEPPER SOUP

BROCCOLI WATERCRESS SOUP

CHINESE TURKEY NOODLE SOUP

CHICKEN BROTH

VEGETABLE BROTH

CHILLED HACKED CHICKEN SALAD

CUCUMBER CRAB SALAD

CRAB AND RICE SALAD IN TOMATO CUPS

SHRIMP AND CRAB SALAD WITH PINE NUT DRESSING

SESAME SHRIMP SALAD

SALMON AND BROCCOLI SALAD

MANDARIN CHICKEN SALAD

NECTARINE TURKEY SALAD WITH ALMONDS

JADE SALAD

SWEET RED PEPPER SALAD

■ Hot and Sour Soup

Makes 6 servings

This is a favorite Chinese restaurant standard. We've simplified it by leaving out some of the hard-to-find traditional ingredients such as tree ears and tiger lily buds, but we think you'll still find it very tasty. You can make this soup more or less "hot" by using a little more or less of the chili pepper.

1/2 cup shredded skinless and boneless chicken breast
1 tablespoon plus 1 teaspoon low-sodium soy sauce
1 teaspoon dry sherry
6 dried Chinese mushrooms, soaked in hot water for 30 minutes
1 carrot, cut into 1/16 × 2-inch shreds
1 cup shredded green cabbage
4 scallions, both white and green parts, shredded
1 to 2 teaspoons minced fresh green chili pepper
4 cups low-sodium chicken broth
2 tablespoons rice vinegar
1/4 teaspoon white pepper
1 tablespoon minced fresh coriander leaves for garnish

1. Combine the chicken, 1 teaspoon soy sauce, and sherry in a small bowl and set aside for 20 to 30 minutes.
2. Drain the mushrooms from their soaking liquid. Remove the tough stems and discard. Cut the mushroom caps into thin shreds.
3. Combine the shredded mushrooms, carrots, cabbage, scallions, and chili pepper in a bowl.
4. Bring the chicken broth, 1 tablespoon soy sauce, rice vinegar, and white pepper to a boil in a saucepan.
5. Add the vegetables and bring to a boil again. Cover and cook for 3 minutes.
6. Remove the cover, stir in the marinated chicken, and cook for 1 minute more.
7. Serve in individual bowls. Garnish with the coriander.

■

Each serving provides:
60 Calories
0.8 g Fat
0.2 g Saturated Fat
16 mg Cholesterol
4 g Carbohydrate
7 g Protein
121 mg Sodium

■

Soups and Salads

■ LOBSTER AND SPINACH SOUP

Makes 4 to 6 servings

This elegant Chinese soup makes an excellent first course for a special dinner.

- 1 tablespoon dry sherry
- 1 tablespoon low-sodium soy sauce
- 1/4 teaspoon white pepper
- 4 cups low-sodium vegetable broth
- 1/2 cup finely chopped onion
- 1 cup sliced fresh mushrooms
- 2 cups fresh spinach, washed and tough stems removed
- 1 cup fresh lobster meat, picked from the shell of a
     1-pound cooked lobster and cut into 3/4-inch pieces
- 1 egg white, lightly beaten
- 1 scallion, both white and green parts, chopped
     for garnish

1. Combine the sherry, soy sauce, and white pepper in a small bowl. Set aside.
2. Bring the vegetable broth to a boil in a saucepan.
3. Add the onion and mushrooms, and bring to a boil again. Cover, reduce the heat to simmer, and cook for 5 minutes.
4. Add the spinach, cover, and cook for 2 minutes.
5. Remove the cover and stir in the sherry mixture.
6. Stir in the lobster meat.
7. Increase the heat to medium. Slowly pour in the beaten egg white while gently stirring the soup with a fork to incorporate the egg into the stock.
8. Ladle the hot soup into individual serving bowls and sprinkle with the scallion. Serve immediately.

> ■
> Each serving provides:
> 68 Calories
> 0.5 g Fat
> 0.1 g Saturated Fat
> 31 mg Cholesterol
> 3 g Carbohydrate
> 7 g Protein
> 174 mg Sodium
> ■

■ CREAMY CORN AND CHICKEN CHOWDER

Makes 4 servings

2 cups low-sodium vegetable or chicken broth
1 can (16 ounces) low-sodium creamed corn
1/2 cup finely chopped green bell pepper
6 to 8 fresh mushrooms, finely chopped
2 teaspoons low-sodium soy sauce
1/2 teaspoon Tabasco
1 Foolproof Poached Chicken breast half, cooked and cubed (see index)
1 scallion, both white and green parts, finely chopped for garnish

1. Combine the broth and the creamed corn in a saucepan and bring to a boil.
2. Add the green pepper, mushrooms, soy sauce, and Tabasco and stir. Cover and cook over medium heat for 3 minutes.
3. Add the chicken and stir to heat through, about 1 minute.
4. Serve in individual bowls and garnish with the scallion.

■

Each serving provides:
191 Calories
3 g Fat
0.7 g Saturated Fat
48 mg Cholesterol
22 g Carbohydrate
20 g Protein
118 mg Sodium

■

■ CHINESE CLAM CHOWDER

Makes 6 servings

This hearty chowder is a good main-dish soup that goes well with a salad or sandwich at lunch or dinner.

2 to 2 1/2 cups low-sodium vegetable or chicken broth
1 can (10 ounces) whole baby clams, drained and
   juice reserved
1 can (8 ounces) tomato sauce
1 teaspoon minced fresh ginger
1 teaspoon minced fresh garlic
1/2 cup finely chopped onion
12 to 14 fresh mushrooms, thinly sliced
1 cup Chinese-Style Boiled Rice (see index)
1 cup coarsely chopped bean sprouts
1 cup frozen green peas, thawed
3 tablespoons chopped fresh parsley
1 tablespoon dry sherry

1. Add enough of the broth to the reserved clam juice to make 3 cups.
2. Bring the clam juice mixture and tomato sauce to a boil in a large saucepan.
3. Add the ginger, garlic, onion, and mushrooms. Cover and cook over medium-low heat for 5 minutes.
4. Add the rice, clams, bean sprouts, and peas. Cook for an additional 3 minutes.
5. Add the parsley and sherry, stir, and serve.

■

Each serving provides:
203 Calories
0.7 g Fat
0.2 g Saturated Fat
32 mg Cholesterol
38 g Carbohydrate
11 g Protein
286 mg Sodium

■

■ WONTON SOUP

Makes 6 servings

This classic Chinese soup takes special effort to make the wontons, but as Confucius might have said, we can't expect all good things to be easy.

6 cups low-sodium chicken broth
1 cup sliced fresh mushrooms
1/4 cup sliced water chestnuts
18 cooked Turkey Wontons (see index)
6 ounces fresh spinach, washed, tough stems removed, cut into shreds
1 tablespoon low-sodium soy sauce
1/4 teaspoon white pepper
1 tablespoon chopped fresh chives for garnish

1. Bring the chicken broth to a boil in a large stockpot.
2. Add the mushrooms. Cover, lower the heat to simmer, and cook for 5 minutes.
3. Add the water chestnuts and the wontons. Cover and cook for 5 minutes.
4. Add the spinach, stir, and cook for 2 minutes.
5. Stir in the soy sauce and white pepper.
6. Serve in individual bowls and garnish with the chives.

■

Each serving provides:
220 Calories
4 g Fat
0.7 g Saturated Fat
25 mg Cholesterol
8 g Carbohydrate
16 g Protein
326 mg Sodium

■

SOUPS AND SALADS

■ CURRIED BUTTERNUT SQUASH SOUP WITH SHRIMP AND CORIANDER

Makes 6 servings

This peppy soup is a good choice for the appetizer course of a small dinner party.

- 4 cups low-sodium chicken broth
- 1 butternut squash (about 1 1/4 pounds), peeled, seeded, and cut into 2-inch chunks
- 1 teaspoon curry powder
- 1 teaspoon fresh lemon juice
- 1/4 teaspoon cayenne pepper
- 1 tablespoon minced fresh coriander leaves, or 1/2 teaspoon dried
- 36 small cooked shrimp, peeled and deveined
- 6 fresh coriander sprigs for garnish

1. Bring the chicken broth to a boil in a saucepan.
2. Add the squash, cover, and cook over medium heat for 12 to 15 minutes, or until the squash is tender.
3. Purée the soup in batches in a blender or food processor.
4. Return the purée to the saucepan and bring to a boil.
5. Add the curry powder, lemon juice, cayenne pepper, and minced coriander. Cover and cook over low heat for about 20 minutes.
6. To serve, place 6 shrimp in the bottom of each soup bowl.
7. Pour the hot soup over the shrimp and garnish each bowl with a fresh coriander sprig.

■

Each serving provides:
60 Calories
0.8 g Fat
0.1 g Saturated Fat
58 mg Cholesterol
5 g Carbohydrate
8 g Protein
80 mg Sodium

■

■ Hot Pepper Soup

Makes 4 to 6 servings

3 large red bell peppers
3 cups low-sodium vegetable or chicken broth
1 can (8 ounces) tomato sauce
1 cup chopped onion
1 teaspoon minced fresh garlic
1 teaspoon minced fresh ginger
1 tablespoon minced fresh green chili pepper
1 tablespoon chopped fresh chives for garnish

1. Preheat the oven to broil.
2. Broil the bell peppers, whole, on a rack on a baking sheet 3 inches from the heat. Turn the peppers as the skin blisters and blackens. It will take about 8 to 10 minutes to blacken the entire pepper. Remove the peppers from the oven, transfer them to a brown paper bag, and close tightly. Open the bag after 10 to 15 minutes and remove the peppers. Slip off and discard the skin. (Don't worry if all the charred skin doesn't come off. This will add flavor to the soup.) Cut the skinned peppers in half and remove the seeds and ribs.
3. Combine all the ingredients except the chives in a large saucepan.
4. Bring to a boil, cover, and cook over medium-low heat for 10 minutes.
5. Pour the soup into the bowl of a food processor or blender and purée, in batches if necessary, until smooth. Set soup aside in the refrigerator until ready to serve.
6. Reheat the soup or serve chilled in individual bowls. Garnish each bowl with the chives.

■

Each serving provides:
52 Calories
0.4 g Fat
0.1 g Saturated Fat
0 mg Cholesterol
10 g Carbohydrate
2 g Protein
240 mg Sodium

■

■ Broccoli Watercress Soup

Makes 4 to 6 servings

This puréed soup has very little fat but has the rich texture of a cream soup, and the subtle taste of watercress.

- 4 cups fresh broccoli florets
- 1 bunch watercress, washed and tough stems removed
- 1/2 cup chopped onion
- 1 teaspoon minced fresh garlic
- 2 cups low-sodium vegetable or chicken broth
- 1 tablespoon dry sherry

1. Pick out enough small broccoli florets to make 1 cup and set aside.
2. Combine the remaining broccoli florets, the watercress, onion, garlic, broth, and sherry in a large saucepan and bring to a boil. Cover, reduce heat to simmer, and cook for 20 minutes.
3. Purée the soup, in batches if necessary, in a blender or food processor.
4. Return the puréed soup to the saucepan and bring to a boil.
5. Add the reserved cup broccoli florets and simmer for 5 minutes, or until tender.
6. Stir in the sherry and ladle into individual bowls.

> ■
>
> Each serving provides:
> 28 Calories
> 0.3 g Fat
> 0.1 g Saturated Fat
> 0 mg Cholesterol
> 5 g Carbohydrate
> 2 g Protein
> 25 mg Sodium
>
> ■

CHINESE TURKEY NOODLE SOUP

Makes 6 servings

Cellophane noodles and soy sauce give this soup its Chinese look and flavor.

8 ounces skinless and boneless fresh turkey breast
1 tablespoon plus 1 teaspoon low-sodium soy sauce
1 teaspoon dry sherry
2 ounces cellophane noodles
6 cups low-sodium chicken broth
1 cup coarsely chopped broccoli florets
1 teaspoon minced fresh green chili pepper
1 teaspoon minced fresh ginger
1/2 cup chopped scallions, both white and green parts
1/4 cup chopped fresh coriander leaves

1. Cut the turkey into thin strips, 1/8 inch wide × 2 inches long.
2. Combine 1 teaspoon soy sauce and the sherry in a bowl.
3. Add the turkey to the bowl and let marinate for 20 to 30 minutes.
4. Place the noodles in a large bowl and pour over boiling water to cover. Set aside for 10 minutes, then drain. Rinse noodles in cold water and drain well. Set aside.
5. Combine the chicken broth, broccoli, chili pepper, ginger, and 1 tablespoon soy sauce in a large saucepan and bring to a boil. Cover, reduce heat to medium, and cook for 5 minutes.
6. Remove the cover and add the turkey. Stir and cook for 30 seconds.
7. Add the noodles and cook for 30 seconds.
8. Stir in the scallions and coriander. Remove from the heat and serve in individual soup bowls.

Each serving provides:
116 Calories
1.5 g Fat
0.4 g Saturated Fat
25 mg Cholesterol
10 g Carbohydrate
13 g Protein
137 mg Sodium

■ CHICKEN BROTH

Makes about 2 quarts

Chicken broth is used in many Chinese recipes. This homemade version is much lower in sodium than most store-bought brands, even those touted as low-sodium. We use this homemade chicken broth or a very low sodium packaged broth with the brand name Herb-Ox.

About 4 pounds chicken bones and parts
    (wings, backs, necks)
10 cups water
 2 large onions, peeled and quartered
 2 large carrots, peeled and sliced
 2 celery stalks with leaves, sliced
1/2 cup tightly packed parsley with stems
 1 tablespoon fresh thyme leaves, or 1 teaspoon dried
 1 bay leaf
 4 garlic cloves, peeled and lightly crushed
 8 to 10 whole peppercorns
 1 tablespoon low-sodium soy sauce

1. Rinse the chicken and remove any excess fat, but leave the skin on the pieces.
2. Combine all the ingredients in a large heavy stockpot and bring to a boil.
3. Partially cover, reduce the heat to low, and simmer for 1 hour. Occasionally skim the foam that accumulates at the top of the pot.
4. Remove the pot from the heat and let the broth cool slightly, then pour it through a sieve lined with cheesecloth or a heavy white paper towel.
5. Refrigerate overnight to allow the fat to harden on the top. Remove the fat and discard.
6. Broth can be stored in the refrigerator for 3 to 4 days, or up to 6 months in the freezer.

■

Each 1-cup serving
  provides:
50 Calories
2 g Fat
0.3 g Saturated Fat
5 mg Cholesterol
3 g Carbohydrate
5 g Protein
20 mg Sodium

■

■ VEGETABLE BROTH

Makes about 2 quarts

Commercially made vegetable broths, like chicken broths, usually have a very high salt content. Just look at the labels. If you wish to use a low-sodium version, here is one you can make yourself.

8 cups water
1 cup dry white wine
4 large onions, peeled and quartered
6 large carrots, peeled and sliced
4 celery stalks with leaves, sliced
1 large parsnip, peeled and sliced
1 cup tightly packed parsley with stems
1 tablespoon fresh thyme leaves, or 1 teaspoon dried
3 bay leaves
5 garlic cloves, peeled and lightly crushed
8 to 10 whole black peppercorns
2 teaspoons low-sodium soy sauce

1. Combine all the ingredients in a large heavy stock-pot and bring to a boil.
2. Partially cover, reduce the heat to low, and simmer for 1 hour.
3. Strain out the vegetables. Taste. If the flavor seems weak, boil uncovered to reduce the broth. (This will make it more flavorful.)
4. Broth can be stored in the refrigerator for 3 to 4 days, or up to 6 months in the freezer.

■

Each 1-cup serving
  provides:
57 Calories
0.2 g Fat
0 g Saturated Fat
0 mg Cholesterol
11 g Carbohydrate
2 g Protein
51 mg Sodium

■

62

■ CHILLED HACKED CHICKEN SALAD

Makes 3 to 4 servings

This popular Chinese restaurant dish makes a good supper choice for a warm summer evening at home. The cucumber releases liquid, so the salad will be juicier if it's made a few hours before you're planning to serve it.

2 carrots, cut into thin strips, 1/8 inch wide × 2 inches long

1 medium cucumber, peeled, cut in half lengthwise, seeds removed and cut into thin strips, 1/8 inch wide × 2 inches long

2 (8-ounce) Foolproof Poached Chicken breast halves, shredded (see index)

3/4 cup Spicy Peanut Sauce (see index)

6 to 8 lettuce leaves, washed and dried

1 tablespoon chopped fresh coriander leaves for garnish

1. Bring water to a boil in a small saucepan and cook the carrots for 2 minutes. Drain and rinse in cold water. Drain again.
2. Combine the carrots, cucumber, and chicken in a large bowl.
3. Add the spicy peanut sauce to the chicken mixture and mix well.
4. Arrange the lettuce leaves on a serving platter.
5. Spoon the salad attractively on top of the lettuce and sprinkle with the coriander.

■

Each serving provides:
290 Calories
10 g Fat
2 g Saturated Fat
72 mg Cholesterol
16 g Carbohydrate
28 g Protein
348 mg Sodium

■

■ CUCUMBER CRAB SALAD

Makes 4 to 6 servings

This elegant salad is perfect for a small dinner party.

  2 medium cucumbers
  1 teaspoon salt
  2 cups small broccoli florets

Crab Mixture
  8 ounces crabmeat, flaked
  2 scallions, both white and green parts, finely chopped
  1 tablespoon minced fresh green chili pepper
  4 red radishes, finely chopped
  1/4 cup finely chopped water chestnuts

Dressing
  1/2 cup rice vinegar
  1/4 cup sugar

Garnish
  1 tablespoon chopped fresh parsley

1. Partially peel the cucumbers, leaving on some of the green skin in alternating strips. Thinly slice the cucumbers into rounds. Place the cucumber slices in a colander and sprinkle with the salt. Toss well. Set aside for 30 minutes.
2. Bring a quart of water to a boil in a saucepan. Add the broccoli and cook for just 1 minute after the water returns to a boil. Drain and rinse the broccoli under cold water to stop the cooking. Set aside in a bowl.
3. Combine the crab mixture ingredients in a bowl. Set aside.
4. Combine the dressing ingredients in a small bowl and stir well, until the sugar is dissolved. Set aside.

■

Each serving provides:
101 Calories
0.6 g Fat
0.1 g Saturated Fat
34 mg Cholesterol
13 g Carbohydrate
9 g Protein
140 mg Sodium

■

5. Rinse the cucumbers to remove the salt and drain. Place the cucumbers in a clean tea towel and squeeze to remove excess moisture. (They will be limp.) Place in a small bowl.
6. Toss 2 tablespoons of the dressing with the cucumbers. Set aside.
7. Toss 4 tablespoons of the dressing with the broccoli florets. Set aside.
8. Toss the remaining dressing with the crab mixture.
9. To serve, place a small mound of the marinated cucumbers on one-third of each salad plate. Next, place a small mound of the broccoli florets next to the cucumbers. Arrange the crab mixture on the remaining third of each plate. Be careful to keep each item separate. Garnish by sprinkling the parsley over the top.

CRAB AND RICE SALAD IN TOMATO CUPS

Makes 8 servings

Our friend Ginger grew up in New York City and remembers this salad from her youth. Tucking the crab and rice mixture into tomatoes is a recent innovation.

Crab Mixture
2 cups flaked crabmeat
2 cups Chinese-Style Boiled Rice (see index)
1/4 cup frozen green peas, thawed
1/4 cup chopped celery
1/4 cup chopped scallions, both white and green parts
1/4 cup chopped green bell pepper
1/4 cup grated carrots
1/4 cup chopped fresh parsley
1 teaspoon minced fresh ginger
1 teaspoon minced fresh garlic
1 teaspoon minced fresh green chili pepper
1 tablespoon chopped fresh basil, or 1 teaspoon dried

Dressing
1/4 cup frozen lemonade concentrate
1 tablespoon low-sodium soy sauce
1 tablespoon rice vinegar
1 teaspoon sesame oil

Additional Ingredients
8 medium-size ripe tomatoes
8 lettuce leaves, washed and dried
8 parsley sprigs for garnish

Each serving provides:
101 Calories
1 g Fat
0.2 g Saturated Fat
32 mg Cholesterol
19 g Carbohydrate
9 g Protein
125 mg Sodium

1. Combine the crab mixture ingredients in a large bowl and mix well.
2. Combine the dressing ingredients in a small bowl and mix well. Toss with the crab mixture. Cover and refrigerate overnight to allow the flavors to blend.
3. Slice off the tops of the tomatoes and scoop out the seeds, juice, and loose pulp. Mix the pulp with the dressed crab mixture. Turn the tomatoes upside-down on paper towels to drain.
4. Fill each tomato with one-eighth of the crab mixture, forming a mound in the center.
5. Arrange a lettuce leaf on each salad plate and place a filled tomato cup on top.
6. Garnish the top of each tomato with a sprig of parsley.

NOTE   For a sophisticated presentation, decorate each plate with 2 Scallion Brushes and a Radish Flower (see index).

SHRIMP AND CRAB SALAD WITH PINE NUT DRESSING

Makes 6 to 8 servings

The dressing for this salad has the look and consistency of a creamy garden dressing but has no cream or eggs—and thus a minimum of fat.

Salad

- 8 ounces medium shrimp (about 20 to 24), peeled and deveined
- 1 medium yellow summer squash, cut into $1/8 \times 2$-inch julienne
- 1 medium green zucchini, cut into $1/8 \times 2$-inch julienne
- 2 cups fresh green beans, trimmed and cut into thin julienne
- 8 ounces crabmeat, flaked
- 1 medium green bell pepper, seeds and ribs removed, cut into $1/8 \times 2$-inch julienne

Dressing

- 1 cup tightly packed fresh coriander leaves
- 1 cup tightly packed fresh parsley
- 1/2 cup pine nuts, lightly browned in a dry skillet over medium heat
- 1 tablespoon minced fresh ginger
- 1 tablespoon minced fresh garlic
- 2 teaspoons minced fresh green chili pepper
- 1/2 cup chopped red onion
- 2 tablespoons low-sodium soy sauce
- 2 tablespoons fresh lemon juice
- 1 tablespoon sesame oil
- 1/2 to 3/4 cup low-sodium vegetable or chicken broth

Additional Ingredients

- 8 lettuce leaves, washed and dried

1. Place each salad ingredient in a separate bowl and set aside.
2. Combine all the dressing ingredients, except the broth, in a food processor or blender and process until smooth. Add just enough broth to give the dressing the consistency of heavy cream. Set aside.
3. Bring water to a boil in a 3 to 4 quart saucepan. Add the shrimp, bring the water to a boil again and cook 1 minute. Remove the shrimp from the pan and drain. Set aside in a large bowl.
4. Bring fresh water to a boil, add the summer squash and the zucchini. When the water comes to a boil again, cook for 30 seconds. Drain and rinse the squash under cold water to stop the cooking process. Drain again. Add the squash to the bowl with the shrimp.
5. Bring the water back to a boil and add the green beans. After the water has come to a boil again, cook the beans for 3 minutes. Drain and rinse under cold water. Drain again. Add to the shrimp bowl.
6. Add the crabmeat and the uncooked green pepper strips to the shrimp bowl.
7. Pour the pine nut dressing over the shrimp mixture and toss well to combine. Cover and refrigerate until ready to serve.
8. To serve, arrange the lettuce leaves on a serving platter and top with the salad.

■
Each serving provides:
210 Calories
7 g Fat
1 g Saturated Fat
79 mg Cholesterol
24 g Carbohydrate
17 g Protein
277 mg Sodium
■

■ SESAME SHRIMP SALAD

Makes 6 servings

Marinade
- 1 teaspoon minced fresh garlic
- 1 tablespoon low-sodium soy sauce
- 1 tablespoon dry sherry

Shrimp
- 24 large shrimp (about 1 pound), peeled and deveined

Fruit Mixture
- 2 mangoes, peeled, pitted, and cut into 1-inch pieces
- 2 cups fresh pineapple, peeled, cored, and cut into 1-inch pieces
- 2 teaspoons minced fresh green chili pepper
- 2 tablespoons chopped scallions
- 2 tablespoons chopped fresh coriander leaves

Dressing
- 1/4 cup frozen pineapple juice concentrate
- 1 teaspoon minced fresh ginger
- 2 tablespoons rice vinegar

Additional Ingredients
- 2 egg whites, lightly beaten
- 1/4 cup sesame seeds, lightly browned in a dry skillet over medium heat
- Canola oil spray
- 6 cups shredded crisp lettuce
- 1 lemon

1. Combine the marinade ingredients in a bowl.
2. Add the shrimp to the bowl and let marinate for 20 to 30 minutes.
3. Combine the fruit mixture ingredients in a large bowl and mix well. Set aside.

■
Each serving provides:
214 Calories
5 g Fat
0.7 g Saturated Fat
53 mg Cholesterol
38 g Carbohydrate
10 g Protein
136 mg Sodium

■

4. Combine the dressing ingredients in a small bowl. Set aside.

5. Preheat the oven to 450°.

6. Dip each shrimp in the egg white first, then in the sesame seeds. (Do not try to coat the entire shrimp with the seeds. A light sprinkling will do.)

7. Spray a baking sheet with the canola oil spray and place the shrimp on the sheet.

8. Bake for 3 minutes, turn over the shrimp, and cook for 3 minutes more.

9. Combine the fruit mixture with the dressing and mix well.

10. To serve, arrange 1 cup of the shredded lettuce on each salad plate. Spoon one-sixth of the fruit mixture on top of the lettuce. Arrange 4 cooked shrimp around the edge of each plate and squeeze the juice of the lemon over the shrimp. Serve while the shrimp are still warm.

Salmon and Broccoli Salad

Makes 3 to 4 servings

The contents and presentation of this unusual salad make it a good choice for a special-occasion luncheon.

2 teaspoons low-sodium soy sauce
1 teaspoon minced fresh ginger
1 teaspoon minced fresh garlic
12 ounces salmon filet, 1 inch thick, with bones and
   skin removed
1 large cucumber, peeled, cut in half lengthwise, seeded,
   and cut into 1/4-inch slices (about 2 cups)
16 small broccoli florets (about 2 cups)
2 tablespoons chopped fresh parsley
1/2 cup coarsely chopped red radishes

Dressing
1/4 cup reserved cooking liquid from steaming salmon
   and vegetables
2 tablespoons frozen lemonade concentrate
1 tablespoon rice vinegar
1 tablespoon low-sodium soy sauce

Garnish
Zest of 1 lemon
1 tablespoon chopped fresh chives

1. Combine the soy sauce, ginger, and garlic in a bowl.
2. Add the salmon and let marinate for 20 to 30 minutes.
3. Place the vegetables in separate bowls.
4. Bring 4 to 6 cups of water to a boil in a wok.
5. On a heatproof platter that will fit in the rack of a bamboo steamer, arrange the cucumber, broccoli, and salmon. Place the broccoli around the edge of the platter, stem ends toward the center. Place the cucumber in the center and top with the salmon. Cover the steamer. (You may need to divide the ingredients between two steamer racks if they don't fit on one.)
6. Place the steamer in the wok over boiling water, cover, and steam for 10 minutes. Remove the wok and steamer from the heat.
7. When cool enough to handle (about 2 minutes), remove the platter from the steamer and drain the liquid, reserving 1/4 cup. Combine the 1/4 cup liquid with the lemonade concentrate, rice vinegar, and soy sauce and set aside.
8. Cover the platter with plastic wrap and refrigerate for at least 1 hour, or until well chilled.
9. Drain the broccoli and place in a small bowl. Toss with 2 tablespoons of the dressing.
10. Drain the cucumbers and place in a small bowl. Toss with 2 tablespoons of the dressing. Add the parsley and radishes and toss to combine.
11. On an oval serving platter, arrange the broccoli at one end and the cucumbers at the other. Place the salmon in the center. Sprinkle the lemon zest over the broccoli and the chives over the salmon. Serve.

Each serving provides:
153 Calories
5 g Fat
1 g Saturated Fat
32 mg Cholesterol
7 g Carbohydrate
20 g Protein
218 mg Sodium

SOUPS AND SALADS

■ MANDARIN CHICKEN SALAD

Makes 6 to 8 servings

This substantial salad makes a great main dish at a luncheon or a summer supper.

Dressing
1/2 cup low-sodium chicken broth

2 tablespoons low-sodium soy sauce

1 tablespoon dry sherry

1 tablespoon minced fresh ginger

1 tablespoon minced fresh garlic

2 teaspoons sugar

2 teaspoons sesame oil

1 teaspoon chili paste

Rice
4 cups Chinese-Style Boiled Rice (see index)

Marinade
1 teaspoon minced fresh ginger

1 teaspoon minced fresh garlic

1 tablespoon low-sodium soy sauce

1 tablespoon dry sherry

Additional Ingredients
3 skinless and boneless chicken breast halves
(18 ounces), fat removed

3/4 cup fresh snow peas, stems and strings removed

1/2 cup chopped scallions

1/2 bunch fresh watercress, tough stems removed, torn
into bite-size pieces

8 water chestnuts, coarsely chopped

1 can (11 ounces) mandarin oranges in light syrup, drained
Canola oil spray

2 cups low-sodium chicken broth

2 tablespoons pine nuts, lightly browned in a dry skillet
over medium heat, for garnish

1. Combine the dressing ingredients with the rice and toss well. Cover and refrigerate overnight to allow the flavors to blend.
2. Combine the marinade ingredients in a shallow dish and mix well.
3. Add the chicken to the dish and let marinate for 20 to 30 minutes.
4. Bring water to a boil in a saucepan. Add the snow peas and cook for 10 seconds. Drain and cool in ice water. Drain well.
5. Combine the snow peas, scallions, watercress, water chestnuts, and mandarin oranges and add to the rice mixture. Set aside.
6. Heat a nonstick skillet over high heat.
7. Carefully spray the skillet with the canola oil spray. (If you have a gas stove, turn off the burner before you spray the skillet.)
8. Add the chicken breasts with marinade and brown for 1 minute on each side.
9. Pour in the chicken broth, cover, reduce the heat to medium-low, and cook for 5 minutes.
10. Remove the skillet from the burner and set aside for 2 minutes.
11. Remove the chicken from the broth (see note) and slice each breast across the grain into 8 slices.
12. Spoon the rice mixture onto a serving platter. Place the slices of chicken on top of the rice and sprinkle with the pine nuts.

NOTE   Refrigerate the remaining chicken broth to use in soup or another recipe.

■

Each serving provides:
302 Calories
5 g Fat
1 g Saturated Fat
54 mg Cholesterol
39 g Carbohydrate
25 g Protein
278 mg Sodium

■

■ NECTARINE TURKEY SALAD WITH ALMONDS

Makes 6 servings

1 pound Shanghai-Style Braised Turkey Breast, cut into
   1-inch pieces (see index)
2 fresh ripe nectarines, peeled and cut into 1-inch pieces
1 cucumber, peeled, cut in half lengthwise and seeds
   removed, cut into 1-inch pieces
1/2 cup thinly sliced scallions, both white and green parts
1 teaspoon minced fresh green chili pepper

Dressing
2 tablespoons hoisin sauce
2 tablespoons chutney
2 tablespoons orange juice
2 tablespoons ketchup
1 tablespoon dry sherry
1 teaspoon chili paste

Additional Ingredients
6 to 8 lettuce leaves, washed and dried
1/4 cup sliced almonds, lightly browned in a dry skillet
   over medium heat, for garnish

1. Combine the turkey, nectarines, cucumber, scallion,
   and chili pepper in a large bowl.
2. Combine the dressing ingredients in a small bowl
   and mix well. Stir the dressing into the turkey
   mixture.
3. Arrange the lettuce leaves on a serving platter.
   Spoon the turkey salad on top and sprinkle with
   the almonds.

■

Each serving provides:
287 Calories
7 g Fat
1 g Saturated Fat
79 mg Cholesterol
18 g Carbohydrate
40 g Protein
186 mg Sodium

■

■ JADE SALAD

Makes 6 servings

Jade green is a popular Chinese color, hence the name of this green salad.

2 cups fresh snow peas, stems and strings removed, cut
    in half on the diagonal
3 to 4 large broccoli stems, peeled and sliced in
    1/2-inch rounds
1/2 cup finely chopped green bell pepper
1/4 cup chopped scallions
2 tablespoons finely chopped fresh parsley

Dressing
2 tablespoons low-sodium soy sauce
2 tablespoons rice vinegar
1 tablespoon sesame oil
1/2 teaspoon Chinese hot oil
1 teaspoon sugar
1/2 teaspoon minced fresh ginger

1. Bring water to a boil in a saucepan. Add the snow peas and cook for 10 seconds. Drain and place in a bowl of ice water to cool and crisp them. Drain and set aside.
2. Bring the water to a boil again, add the broccoli stems, and cook for 30 seconds. Drain and place in a bowl of ice water. Drain.
3. Combine the snow peas, broccoli, green pepper, scallions, and parsley in a bowl. Cover and refrigerate until ready to serve.
4. Combine the dressing ingredients and mix well.
5. Toss the dressing with the vegetables just before serving.

> ■
> Each serving provides:
> 60 Calories
> 3 g Fat
> 0.4 g Saturated Fat
> 0 mg Cholesterol
> 7 g Carbohydrate
> 3 g Protein
> 141 mg Sodium
> ■

■ SWEET RED PEPPER SALAD

Makes 4 to 6 servings

The dressing—rice vinegar, Chinese hot oil, and soy sauce—gives this salad its Chinese character. The peppers and greens give it a bright, fresh look.

Dressing

2 tablespoons rice vinegar

1/2 teaspoon Chinese hot oil

1/2 teaspoon low-sodium soy sauce

1/2 teaspoon sugar

Salad

3 large red bell peppers cut in half lengthwise, seeds and ribs removed

4 ounces mustard greens or arugula, rinsed and torn into bite-size pieces

1 cucumber, peeled, cut in half lengthwise, seeded, and cut into 1/2-inch slices

3 tablespoons chopped scallions

Garnish

1 tablespoon chopped fresh coriander leaves

1. Combine the dressing ingredients in a small bowl. Mix well, until the sugar is dissolved. Set aside.
2. Preheat the oven to broil.
3. Place the red pepper halves skin-side up on the broiler pan, about 3 inches from the heat. Broil until the skin blackens and blisters, about 5 minutes.

■

Each serving provides:

23 Calories

0.6 g Fat

0.1 g Saturated Fat

0 mg Cholesterol

4 g Carbohydrate

1 g Protein

20 mg Sodium

■

---

4. Remove the peppers from the heat and let cool slightly. Peel off the skin from the peppers. Most of the blackened skin will easily peel off. Cut the peeled peppers into 1-inch squares.
5. Pour the dressing over the peppers while they are still warm. Set aside for 30 minutes or longer.
6. When ready to serve the salad, toss the mustard greens, cucumbers, and scallions with the peppers.
7. Serve on individual plates and garnish with the coriander.

SIX

Vegetables

Stir-Fried Asparagus

Green and Yellow Squash with Carrots

Spicy Szechuan Eggplant

Eggplant and Broccoli

Carrots with Orange, Ginger, and Cumin

Stir-Fried Snow Peas

Szechuan Green Beans

Dry-Cooked Green Beans

Spinach and Yellow Squash

Spicy Stir-Fried Broccoli

Sautéed Spinach with Garlic, Onions, and Tomato

■ Stir-Fried Asparagus

Makes 4 servings

On Your Tray

- Canola oil spray
- Bowl of seasonings
- Bowl of asparagus
- Bowl of sauce
- Cornstarch mixture

Seasonings

1/2 cup finely chopped onion
1 tablespoon minced fresh garlic

Sauce

1 cup low-sodium vegetable or chicken broth
2 tablespoons low-sodium soy sauce
2 tablespoons dry sherry

Asparagus

1 pound asparagus, trimmed and cut into 2-inch pieces on the diagonal

Additional Ingredients

1 tablespoon cornstarch dissolved in 2 tablespoons cold water
Canola oil spray

Preparation

1. Combine the seasoning ingredients in a small bowl.
2. Combine the sauce ingredients in another small bowl.
3. Assemble your cooking tray.

Cooking

1. Heat a nonstick wok over high heat for 2 minutes.
2. Carefully spray the wok with the canola oil spray. (If you have a gas stove, turn off the burner before you spray the wok.) Add the seasonings and stir-fry for 30 seconds.

3. Add the asparagus and stir-fry for 30 seconds.
4. Add the sauce, cover, turn heat to medium-low, and cook for 3 minutes.
5. Remove the cover and return to high heat. Pour in the cornstarch mixture and stir to thicken the sauce, about 30 seconds.
6. Remove from the wok and serve.

Each serving provides:
61 Calories
0.5 g Fat
0.2 g Saturated Fat
0 mg Cholesterol
11 g Carbohydrate
4 g Protein
205 mg Sodium

■ GREEN AND YELLOW SQUASH WITH CARROTS

Makes 6 servings

2 medium carrots, peeled and cut into $1/8 \times$ 2-inch julienne
1 medium green zucchini, scrubbed and cut into $1/8 \times$ 2-inch julienne
1 medium yellow summer squash, scrubbed and cut into $1/8 \times$ 2-inch julienne

ON YOUR TRAY

- Canola oil spray
- Bowl of seasonings
- Bowl of vegetables
- Bowl of sauce
- Coriander

Seasonings

1 teaspoon minced fresh ginger
1 teaspoon minced fresh garlic

Sauce

$1/4$ cup low-sodium vegetable or chicken broth
2 tablespoons low-sodium soy sauce
1 tablespoon dry sherry

Additional Ingredients

Canola oil spray
1 tablespoon chopped fresh coriander leaves for garnish

Preparation

1. Cook the carrots covered in boiling water for 2 minutes. Drain and rinse in cold water to stop the cooking process. Drain again.
2. Combine the carrots, zucchini, and yellow squash in a bowl.
3. Combine the seasoning ingredients in a small bowl.
4. Combine the sauce ingredients in another small bowl.
5. Assemble your cooking tray.

■

Each serving provides:
33 Calories
0.2 g Fat
0 g Saturated Fat
0 mg Cholesterol
7 g Carbohydrate
2 g Protein
142 mg Sodium

■

Cooking

1. Heat a nonstick wok over high heat for 2 minutes.
2. Carefully spray the wok with the canola oil spray. (If you have a gas stove, turn off the burner before you spray the wok.) Add the seasonings and stir-fry for 15 seconds.
3. Add the vegetables and stir-fry for 2 minutes.
4. Add the sauce, stir, and cover. Turn heat to medium-low and cook for 2 minutes.
5. Remove the vegetables from the wok, sprinkle with the coriander, and serve.

■ Spicy Szechuan Eggplant

Makes 4 to 6 servings

1 medium eggplant, peeled, sliced, and cut into
   $1/2$ inch wide × 2 inches long pieces
1 teaspoon salt
2 stalks celery, thinly sliced on the diagonal
1 medium onion, peeled, cut into thin slices, and
   separated into rings
1 medium red bell pepper, seeds and ribs removed, cut
   into $1/8$ × 1-inch julienne

On Your Tray

- Canola oil spray
- Bowl of seasonings
- Bowl of eggplant
- Bowl of celery
- Bowl of onion
- Bowl of red bell pepper
- Bowl of sauce
- Sesame seeds

Seasonings

1 tablespoon minced fresh garlic
3 scallions, both white and green parts, chopped
1 tablespoon finely chopped fresh green chili pepper

Sauce

1 tablespoon sesame oil
2 tablespoons rice vinegar
$1/2$ teaspoon salt, or to taste
1 teaspoon sugar
$1/2$ teaspoon fennel seeds

Additional Ingredients

Canola oil spray
2 tablespoons sesame seeds for garnish, lightly browned
   in a dry skillet over medium heat

```
■
Each serving provides:
74 Calories
4 g Fat
0.7 g Saturated Fat
0 mg Cholesterol
17 g Carbohydrate
3 g Protein
212 mg Sodium
■
```

Preparation

1. Sprinkle the eggplant with the salt, toss, and place in a colander for 30 minutes to drain. Rinse with cold water, drain, and set aside.
2. Place the celery, onion, and red pepper in separate bowls.

86

3. Combine the seasonings in a small bowl.
4. Combine the sauce ingredients in another small bowl.
5. Assemble your cooking tray.

Cooking

1. Heat a nonstick wok over high heat for 2 minutes.
2. Carefully spray the wok with the canola oil spray. (If you have a gas stove, turn off the burner before you spray the wok.) Add the seasonings and stir-fry for 15 seconds.
3. Add the eggplant and stir-fry for 1 minute.
4. Add the celery and onion and stir-fry for 2 minutes.
5. Add the red pepper and stir-fry for 30 seconds.
6. Add the sauce and stir to mix and heat through, about 30 seconds.
7. Transfer the vegetables to a serving bowl, sprinkle with the sesame seeds, and serve.

■ EGGPLANT AND BROCCOLI

Makes 4 to 6 servings

1 medium eggplant, peeled and cut into 1-inch cubes
  (3 cups)
1 teaspoon salt
2 cups broccoli florets
1 large ripe tomato, peeled and coarsely chopped

Seasonings
1/2 cup finely chopped onion
1 tablespoon minced fresh garlic
1 teaspoon minced fresh ginger

ON YOUR TRAY

- Canola oil spray
- Bowl of seasonings
- Bowl of eggplant
- Bowl of broccoli
- Bowl of tomato
- Bowl of sauce
- Scallions

Sauce
1/2 cup low-sodium vegetable or chicken broth
1 tablespoon dry sherry

Additional Ingredients
  Canola oil spray
1/4 cup chopped scallions, both white and green parts,
  for garnish

Preparation

1. Sprinkle the eggplant with the salt, toss, and place
   in a colander for 30 minutes to drain. Rinse with
   cold water, drain, and set aside.
2. Place the broccoli and tomato in separate bowls.
3. Combine the seasoning ingredients in a small bowl.
4. Combine the sauce ingredients in another small
   bowl.
5. Assemble your cooking tray.

Cooking

1. Heat a nonstick wok over high heat for 2 minutes.
2. Carefully spray the wok with the canola oil spray. (If you have a gas stove, turn off the burner before you spray the wok.) Add the seasonings and stir-fry for 30 seconds.
3. Add the eggplant and stir-fry for 1 minute.
4. Add the broccoli and stir-fry for 1 more minute.
5. Add the tomato and stir.
6. Pour in the sauce, cover, and lower the heat to medium. Cook for 3 minutes.
7. Transfer to a serving platter, sprinkle with the scallions, and serve.

■

Each serving provides:
31 Calories
0.3 g Fat
0.1 g Saturated Fat
0 mg Cholesterol
7 g Carbohydrate
2 g Protein
13 mg Sodium

■

CARROTS WITH ORANGE, GINGER, AND CUMIN

Makes 4 to 6 servings

This easy vegetable side dish gives carrots a whole new personality.

ON YOUR TRAY

- Bowl of carrots and ginger
- Orange juice
- Cumin
- Cornstarch mixture

1 pound carrots, peeled
3 thin slices fresh ginger, each about the size of a quarter
1/2 teaspoon ground cumin
1 1/2 cups orange juice
1 tablespoon cornstarch dissolved in 2 tablespoons cold water

Preparation

1. Cut the carrots into julienne, 1/8 inch wide × 2 inches long. Set aside in a bowl. Add the ginger to the bowl.
2. Assemble your cooking tray.

Cooking

1. Bring the orange juice to a boil in a wok or saucepan.
2. Add the carrot and ginger and cumin to the wok. Bring to a boil again, cover, and lower the heat to simmer. Cook for 2 to 3 minutes, or until the carrots are cooked through but still firm.
3. Strain the carrots and reserve the cooking liquid. Set the carrots aside in a bowl. Discard the ginger slices.
4. Bring the reserved liquid to a boil in the wok and add the cornstarch mixture. Stir until the sauce is thickened.
5. Return the carrots to the pan. Stir to coat the carrots and to heat them through, about 1 minute.

■

Each serving provides:
94 Calories
0.5 g Fat
0.1 g Saturated Fat
0 mg Cholesterol
22 g Carbohydrate
2 g Protein
15 mg Sodium

■

■ STIR-FRIED SNOW PEAS

Makes 3 to 4 servings

Seasonings
- 1 teaspoon minced fresh garlic
- 2 teaspoons minced fresh ginger

Sauce
- 1 teaspoon low-sodium soy sauce
- 1 teaspoon sesame oil

Peas
- 8 ounces fresh snow peas (about 2½ cups), stems and strings removed

Additional Ingredient
- Canola oil spray

On Your Tray
- Canola oil spray
- Bowl of seasonings
- Snow peas
- Bowl of sauce

Preparation

1. Combine the seasoning ingredients in a small bowl.
2. Combine the sauce ingredients in another small bowl.
3. Assemble your cooking tray.

Cooking

1. Heat a nonstick wok over high heat for 2 minutes.
2. Carefully spray the wok with the canola oil spray. (If you have a gas stove, turn off the burner before you spray the wok.) Add the seasonings and stir-fry for 15 seconds.
3. Add the snow peas and stir-fry for 1 minute.
4. Stir in the sauce.
5. Remove from the heat and serve.

■

Each serving provides:
42 Calories
1 g Fat
0.2 g Saturated Fat
0 mg Cholesterol
8 g Carbohydrate
2 g Protein
36 mg Sodium

■

■ SZECHUAN GREEN BEANS

Makes 6 to 8 servings

1 pound fresh green beans, trimmed and cut into
2-inch pieces

Seasoning Mixture

1/4 cup lean ground turkey

1 teaspoon minced fresh ginger

1 teaspoon minced fresh garlic

1/2 cup minced onion

8 water chestnuts, minced

2 tablespoons minced fresh green chili pepper

On Your Tray

- Canola oil spray
- Bowl of seasoning mixture
- Bowl of green beans
- Bowl of sauce

Sauce

1/4 cup low-sodium chicken broth or water

1 tablespoon dry sherry

1 tablespoon low-sodium soy sauce

1 teaspoon sugar

Additional Ingredient

Canola oil spray

Preparation

1. Bring water to a boil in a saucepan. Add the green beans and boil for 3 minutes. Drain and rinse in cold water. Drain and set aside in a bowl.
2. Combine the seasoning mixture ingredients in a bowl.
3. Combine the sauce ingredients in another bowl and mix well, until the sugar is dissolved.
4. Assemble your cooking tray.

Cooking

1. Heat a nonstick wok over high heat for 2 minutes.
2. Carefully spray the wok with the canola oil spray. (If you have a gas stove, turn off the burner before you spray the wok.) Add the seasoning mixture and stir-fry for 1 minute.
3. Add the green beans and stir to combine with the seasoning mixture.
4. Add the sauce, cover, reduce heat to medium, and cook for 2 minutes.
5. Remove from the wok and serve.

■

Each serving provides:
63 Calories
0.6 g Fat
0.2 g Saturated Fat
12 mg Cholesterol
8 g Carbohydrate
6 g Protein
50 mg Sodium

■

■ DRY-COOKED GREEN BEANS

Makes 3 to 4 servings

"Dry-cooked" in this case means cooking the beans covered in a simmering sauce until tender, then uncovering them and increasing the heat until the sauce evaporates and all the flavor is left in the beans.

Seasonings
- 1 tablespoon minced fresh ginger
- 1/4 cup minced onion

ON YOUR TRAY

- Canola oil spray
- Bowl of seasonings
- Bowl of green beans
- Bowl of sauce

Sauce
- 1/2 cup low-sodium vegetable broth or water
- 1 teaspoon sugar
- 1 tablespoon chili paste
- 1/2 teaspoon sesame oil
- 1 tablespoon low-sodium soy sauce

Beans
- 8 ounces fresh green beans, trimmed

Additional Ingredient
- Canola oil spray

Preparation

1. Combine the seasoning ingredients in a small bowl.
2. Combine the sauce ingredients in another small bowl.
3. Cut any large green beans in half.
4. Assemble your cooking tray.

Cooking

1. Heat a nonstick wok over high heat for 2 minutes.
2. Carefully spray the wok with the canola oil spray. (If you have a gas stove, turn off the burner before you spray the wok.) Add the seasonings and stir-fry for 15 seconds.

■

Each serving provides:
41 Calories
0.7 g Fat
0.1 g Saturated Fat
0 mg Cholesterol
8 g Carbohydrate
1 g Protein
307 mg Sodium

■

94

3. Add the green beans and stir-fry for 1 minute.
4. Add the sauce, stir, and cover. Turn heat to low and cook for 6 minutes.
5. Remove the cover, return to high heat and cook, stirring continuously, until the liquid evaporates. This should take about 3 to 4 minutes.
6. Remove from the wok and serve.

SPINACH AND YELLOW SQUASH

Makes 4 servings

10 ounces fresh spinach, washed, tough stems removed, and coarsely chopped
2 cups cubed yellow summer squash
1/4 cup coarsely chopped water chestnuts

Seasonings
1/4 cup finely chopped onion
1 teaspoon minced fresh ginger

Sauce
1 tablespoon low-sodium soy sauce
1 tablespoon dry sherry

Additional Ingredient
Canola oil spray

ON YOUR TRAY

- Canola oil spray
- Bowl of seasonings
- Bowl of yellow squash
- Bowl of spinach
- Bowl of water chestnuts
- Bowl of sauce

Preparation

1. Place the spinach, squash, and water chestnuts in separate bowls.
2. Combine the seasoning ingredients in a small bowl.
3. Combine the sauce ingredients in another small bowl.
4. Assemble your cooking tray.

Cooking

1. Heat a nonstick wok over high heat for 2 minutes.
2. Carefully spray the wok with the canola oil spray. (If you have a gas stove, turn off the burner before you spray the wok.) Add the seasonings and stir-fry for 15 seconds.
3. Add the squash and stir-fry for 1 minute.

4. Add the spinach and water chestnuts and stir-fry for 1 more minute.
5. Stir in the sauce.
6. Remove from the wok and serve.

■

Each serving provides:
36 Calories
0.3 g Fat
0.1 g Saturated Fat
0 mg Cholesterol
7 g Carbohydrate
2 g Protein
123 mg Sodium

■

■ Spicy Stir-Fried Broccoli

Makes 3 to 4 servings

Seasonings
3 to 4 dried red chili peppers, 1 1/2 to 2 inches long
1 tablespoon minced fresh garlic
1 teaspoon minced fresh ginger

On Your Tray

- Canola oil spray
- Bowl of seasonings
- Bowl of broccoli
- Bowl of sauce
- Cornstarch mixture

Sauce
1 cup low-sodium vegetable or chicken broth
2 tablespoons low-sodium soy sauce
1 teaspoon sugar

Broccoli
8 ounces fresh broccoli florets

Additional Ingredients
1 tablespoon cornstarch dissolved in 2 tablespoons
  cold water
Canola oil spray

Preparation

1. Combine the seasoning ingredients in a small bowl.
2. Combine the sauce ingredients in another small bowl.
3. Assemble your cooking tray.

Cooking

1. Heat a nonstick wok over high heat for 2 minutes.
2. Carefully spray the wok with the canola oil spray. (If you have a gas stove, turn off the burner before you spray the wok.) Add the seasonings and stir-fry for 15 seconds.
3. Add the broccoli and stir-fry for 30 seconds.

■

Each serving provides:
48 Calories
0.2 g Fat
0 g Saturated Fat
0 mg Cholesterol
10 g Carbohydrate
2 g Protein
215 mg Sodium

■

VEGETABLES

4. Pour in the sauce and cover. Reduce the heat to medium and cook for 3 to 4 minutes, or until the broccoli is cooked but still crisp.
5. Remove the cover, return to high heat and add the cornstarch mixture. Stir until the sauce is thickened, about 30 seconds.
6. Remove from the wok and discard the red chili peppers before serving.

Sautéed Spinach with Garlic, Onions, and Tomato

Makes 4 servings

1 pound fresh spinach, washed and tough
    stems discarded
1 large ripe tomato, peeled and coarsely chopped

Seasonings
1 medium onion, chopped
2 teaspoons minced fresh garlic

On Your Tray

- Canola oil spray
- Bowl of seasonings
- Bowl of spinach

Additional Ingredients
    Canola oil spray
    Salt and pepper to taste

Preparation

1. Place the spinach and tomato in separate bowls.
2. Combine the seasoning ingredients in a small bowl.
3. Assemble your cooking tray.

Cooking

1. Heat a nonstick wok over high heat for 2 minutes.
2. Carefully spray the wok with the canola oil spray. (If you have a gas stove, turn off the burner before you spray the wok.) Add the seasonings and stir-fry for 30 seconds.

Each serving provides:
29 Calories
0.3 g Fat
0.1 g Saturated Fat
0 mg Cholesterol
6 g Carbohydrate
2 g Protein
37 mg Sodium

3. Add the spinach, a large handful at a time, and turn with a large spatula. As each handful of spinach wilts, add another large handful and continue until all the spinach has been added to the wok.
4. Stir in the tomato.
5. Remove from the heat and add salt and pepper to taste. Serve immediately.

SEVEN

Rice and Noodles

Chinese-Style Boiled Rice

Yang Chow Fried Rice

Shrimp Fried Rice

Spicy Vegetable Fried Rice with Sweet Potatoes

Orange-Minted Fried Rice

Sesame Noodles with Chicken and Cucumber

Pork Lo Mein with Red Cabbage, Green Peas, and Bean Sprouts

Turkey Wontons with Spicy Scallion Sauce

Ants Climbing a Tree

Baby Clams and Noodles in Black Bean Sauce

Land and Sea Noodles

Triple Mushroom Rice Noodles with Turkey

■ CHINESE-STYLE BOILED RICE

Makes 4 to 6 servings

Rice is the heart of the Chinese diet. There is a traditional Chinese greeting, "Have you had your rice today?", that is the equivalent to a Western "How are you?".

In Western cuisines there is nothing really comparable to the importance of rice in China. For many Chinese, except in the North, the day starts with a rice porridge for breakfast. Then it is a rare meal in the rest of the day that does not include rice in some form. Usually this is boiled rice, but there are also fried rice and rice noodles, rice flour, rice wine, rice vinegar, sweet rice, and rice cakes.

It is not surprising that the Chinese take special care in the preparation of rice. Often they use long-grain rice which cooks up to a fluffier, more granular consistency than short-grain rice. We generally use a readily available long-grain brand such as Uncle Ben's or Carolina. Here is an easy way to cook rice in the Chinese style.

2 cups long-grain white rice
3 cups cold water

1. Combine the rice and the water in a 2-quart saucepan (see note).
2. Place the saucepan over high heat. Cover and bring to a boil.
3. When steam begins to escape from under the lid, reduce the heat to low and set a timer for 20 minutes. Do not remove the cover during cooking, or the steam will escape.
4. Turn off the heat but allow the covered saucepan to rest another 20 minutes (see note). Again, do not remove the cover.
5. Before serving, fluff the rice with a fork or chopsticks.

NOTE The Chinese usually rinse the rice grains several times in cold water before cooking to wash off some of the starch. You can do this if you wish, but we haven't found it to be necessary with the rice brands we use. In addition, if the rice remains covered, it will stay warm an additional 30 minutes. This will help your timing if dinner is delayed.

Each serving provides:
170 Calories
0 g Fat
0 g Saturated Fat
0 mg Cholesterol
38 g Carbohydrate
4 g Protein
0 mg Sodium

YANG CHOW FRIED RICE

Makes 6 servings

The city of Yang Chow is noted for its fried rice dishes, and this combination of shrimp, pork, and vegetables is a popular choice. If you wish, you can leave out the shrimp or the pork and substitute chicken or turkey. Fried rice combinations are a good way to use leftover cooked meats and rice.

ON YOUR TRAY

- Canola oil spray
- Bowl of seasonings
- Bowl of carrots
- Bowl of remaining vegetables
- Bowl of sauce
- Bowl of rice
- Bowl of shrimp and pork
- Scallions

Seasonings

2 teaspoons minced fresh garlic
1 cup finely chopped onion

Vegetables

2 medium carrots, peeled and cut into 1/4-inch cubes
2 large broccoli stems, peeled and cut into 1/4-inch cubes
1 small green bell pepper, seeds and ribs removed, and cut into 1/4-inch cubes
8 water chestnuts, cut into 1/4-inch cubes
1 stalk celery, cut into 1/4-inch cubes

Sauce

1/2 cup low-sodium chicken broth
2 tablespoons low-sodium soy sauce
1 tablespoon dry sherry

Additional Ingredients

8 to 10 cooked medium shrimp, diced
1/2 cup 1/4-inch cubed cooked pork or ham
3 cups Chinese-Style Boiled Rice (see index)
3 scallions, both white and green parts, chopped
Canola oil spray

Preparation

1. Combine the seasoning ingredients in a small bowl.
2. Place the carrots in a bowl. Combine the broccoli, green pepper, water chestnuts, and celery in another bowl.
3. Combine the sauce ingredients in a small bowl.
4. Combine the shrimp and pork in another small bowl.
5. Assemble your cooking tray.

Cooking

1. Heat a nonstick wok over high heat for 2 minutes.
2. Carefully spray the wok with the canola oil spray. (If you have a gas stove, turn off the burner before you spray the wok.) Add the seasonings and stir-fry for 30 seconds.
3. Add the carrots and stir-fry for 1 minute.
4. Add the remaining vegetables and stir-fry for 1 minute.
5. Add the sauce, cover, and simmer for 1 minute.
6. Remove the cover, add the rice and the shrimp and pork and stir-fry for 2 minutes to heat through.
7. Stir in the scallions. Remove from the wok and serve.

Each serving provides:
232 Calories
4 g Fat
1 g Saturated Fat
90 mg Cholesterol
28 g Carbohydrate
22 g Protein
229 mg Sodium

■ Shrimp Fried Rice

Makes 4 to 6 servings

6 dried Chinese mushrooms, soaked in hot water for
  30 minutes
1 cup chopped celery
1 cup chopped green bell pepper
1/2 bunch watercress, rinsed, tough stems removed, and
  coarsely chopped
2 cups small shrimp (about 30 to 36), peeled
  and deveined
3 cups Chinese-Style Boiled Rice (see index)

On Your Tray

- Canola oil spray
- Bowl of seasonings
- Bowl of celery
- Bowl of green pepper
- Bowl of mushrooms
- Bowl of watercress
- Bowl of shrimp
- Bowl of rice
- Bowl of sauce
- Scallions
- Coriander

Seasonings
1 tablespoon minced fresh ginger
1 tablespoon minced fresh garlic
1/2 cup finely chopped onion

Sauce
1/4 cup low-sodium chicken broth
3 tablespoons low-sodium soy sauce
2 tablespoons dry sherry

Additional Ingredients
3 tablespoons chopped scallions, both white and
  green parts
2 tablespoons finely chopped fresh coriander leaves
Canola oil spray

Preparation

1. Drain the mushrooms from their soaking liquid.
   Remove the tough stems and discard. Coarsely
   chop the caps. Place chopped mushrooms in a
   small bowl.
2. Place the celery, green pepper, watercress, shrimp,
   and rice in separate bowls.
3. Combine the seasoning ingredients in a small bowl.

4. Combine the sauce ingredients in another small bowl.
5. Assemble your cooking tray.

Cooking

1. Heat a nonstick wok over high heat for 2 minutes.
2. Carefully coat the bottom of the wok with the canola oil spray. (If you have a gas stove, turn off the burner before you spray the wok.) Add the seasonings and stir-fry for 15 seconds.
3. Add the celery and stir-fry for 30 seconds.
4. Add the green pepper and stir-fry for 30 seconds.
5. Add the mushrooms and watercress and stir-fry for 30 seconds.
6. Push the vegetables to the side of the wok and add the shrimp. Stir-fry for 30 seconds.
7. Add the rice and stir to break up any lumps.
8. Pour in the sauce and stir well to combine all the ingredients. Cover and heat rice for about 2 minutes.
9. Uncover and stir in the scallions and coriander. Remove from the wok and serve.

■

Each serving provides:
152 Calories
1 g Fat
0.2 g Saturated Fat
72 mg Cholesterol
24 g Carbohydrate
13 g Protein
228 mg Sodium

■

■ Spicy Vegetable Fried Rice with Sweet Potatoes

Makes 6 servings

On Your Tray

- Canola oil spray
- Bowl of seasonings
- Bowl of vegetables
- Bowl of sauce
- Bowl of rice
- Scallions

Seasonings

1 tablespoon minced fresh ginger
1 tablespoon minced fresh garlic
1 tablespoon minced fresh green chili pepper

Vegetables

1 medium sweet potato, peeled and cut into
    $1/2$-inch cubes
3 ounces fresh green beans, trimmed and cut into
    $1/4$-inch slices
2 stalks celery, cut into $1/4$-inch cubes
1 cup finely chopped onion
1 red bell pepper, seeds and ribs removed, and cut into
    $1/4$-inch squares
1 cup chopped fresh mushrooms

Sauce

$1/2$ cup low-sodium vegetable broth
2 tablespoons low-sodium soy sauce
1 tablespoon dry sherry
1 teaspoon curry powder

Additional Ingredients

3 cups Chinese-Style Boiled Rice (see index)
3 scallions, both white and green parts, chopped
    Canola oil spray

Preparation

1. Combine the seasoning ingredients in a small bowl.
2. Bring water to a boil in a saucepan. Add the sweet potatoes and green beans and boil for 2 minutes. Drain and place in a large bowl.
3. Add the celery, onion, red pepper, and mushrooms to the sweet potatoes and green beans.
4. Combine the sauce ingredients in a small bowl.
5. Assemble your cooking tray.

Cooking

1. Heat a nonstick wok over high heat for 2 minutes.
2. Carefully spray the wok with the canola oil spray. (If you have a gas stove, turn off the burner before you spray the wok.) Add the seasonings and stir-fry for 15 seconds.
3. Add the vegetables and stir-fry for 1 minute.
4. Add the sauce, cover, and cook for 1 minute.
5. Remove the cover, add the rice, and toss well to break up any lumps. Stir-fry for 1 to 2 minutes, or until rice is heated through.
6. Stir in the scallions. Remove from the wok and serve.

> ■
> Each serving provides:
> 149 Calories
> 0.4 g Fat
> 0.1 g Saturated Fat
> 0 mg Cholesterol
> 33 g Carbohydrate
> 4 g Protein
> 158 mg Sodium
> ■

■ ORANGE-MINTED FRIED RICE

Makes 4 to 6 servings

ON YOUR TRAY

- Canola oil spray
- Bowl of seasonings
- Bowl of celery and onion
- Bowl of mushrooms
- Bowl of rice
- Bowl of sauce
- Bowl of scallions and pine nuts
- Mandarin oranges
- Mint

Seasonings

- 1 tablespoon minced fresh ginger
- 1 tablespoon minced fresh garlic

Vegetables

- 1/2 cup chopped celery
- 1/2 cup chopped onion
- 1 cup chopped fresh mushrooms

Sauce

- 1/4 cup frozen orange juice concentrate
- 1 tablespoon low-sodium soy sauce

Additional Ingredients

- 4 scallions, both white and green parts, chopped
- 1/4 cup pine nuts, lightly browned in a dry skillet over medium heat
- 4 cups Chinese-Style Boiled Rice (see index)
- 1/2 cup drained canned mandarin oranges in light syrup for garnish
- 2 tablespoons chopped fresh mint leaves for garnish
  Canola oil spray

■

Each serving provides:
240 Calories
3 g Fat
0.5 g Saturated Fat
0 mg Cholesterol
48 g Carbohydrate
6 g Protein
82 mg Sodium

■

Preparation

1. Combine the seasoning ingredients in a small bowl.
2. Combine the celery and the onion in a bowl. Place the mushrooms in a separate bowl.
3. Combine the sauce ingredients in a small bowl.
4. Combine the scallions and the pine nuts in another small bowl.
5. Assemble your cooking tray.

Cooking

1. Heat a nonstick wok over high heat for 2 minutes.
2. Carefully spray the wok with the canola oil spray.
   (If you have a gas stove, turn off the burner before
   you spray the wok.)
3. Add the seasonings and stir-fry for 15 seconds.
4. Add the celery and onion and stir-fry for 1 minute.
5. Add the mushrooms and stir-fry for 30 seconds.
6. Add the rice and toss well to break up any lumps.
   Stir-fry for 30 seconds.
7. Add the sauce and stir-fry for 30 seconds.
8. Add the scallions and pine nuts and stir-fry for
   30 seconds.
9. Transfer to a serving bowl. Decoratively arrange
   the oranges on top of the rice and sprinkle with
   the mint.

SESAME NOODLES WITH CHICKEN AND CUCUMBER

Makes 3 to 4 servings

Sesame noodles usually are served at room temperature. Their distinctive nutty taste is a classic Chinese flavor. This version of the popular dish includes chicken and cucumber.

8 ounces thin Chinese egg noodles, cooked and drained
1 teaspoon minced fresh ginger
1 tablespoon minced fresh garlic
3 to 4 dried red chilies, each 1 1/2 to 2 inches long
1 cup coarsely chopped onion

ON YOUR TRAY

- Canola oil spray
- Bowl of chilies
- Bowl of onion
- Bowl of garlic and ginger
- Bowl of sauce
- Bowl of noodles
- Bowl of scallions
- Bowl of chicken
- Bowl of cucumbers
- Sesame seeds

Sauce

1/2 cup low-sodium chicken broth
3 tablespoons oyster sauce
2 tablespoons rice vinegar
1 tablespoon low-sodium soy sauce
1 tablespoon sesame oil
1 tablespoon sugar

Additional Ingredients

2 Foolproof Poached Chicken breast halves (see index)
1 medium cucumber, peeled, cut in half lengthwise, and seeds removed
6 scallions, both white and green parts, thinly sliced
1 tablespoon sesame seeds, lightly browned in a dry skillet over medium heat, for garnish
Canola oil spray

Preparation

1. Place the noodles in a bowl with 1/4 cup of cold water to prevent them from sticking.
2. Combine the ginger and garlic in a small bowl. Put the chilies and onion in separate bowls.

3. Combine the sauce ingredients in a bowl and stir well, until the sugar is dissolved.
4. Cut the chicken across the grain into $1/8$-inch slices and then cut each slice into thin slivers. Place in a bowl.
5. Cut the cucumber into slivers, $1/8$ inch thick $\times$ 2 inches long. Place in a bowl.
6. Assemble your cooking tray.

Cooking

1. Heat a nonstick wok over high heat for 2 minutes.
2. Carefully spray the wok with the canola oil spray. (If you have a gas stove, turn off the burner before you spray the wok.)
3. Add the chilies and stir-fry for 15 seconds.
4. Add the onion and stir-fry for 30 seconds.
5. Add the garlic and ginger and stir-fry for another 30 seconds.
6. Add the sauce, then the noodles, and stir. Cover and cook over medium heat for $1^{1}/_{2}$ minutes.
7. Transfer contents of the wok to a large serving bowl. Add the scallions and toss well to mix. Remove and discard the dried chilies.
8. Top the noodles with the slivered chicken and cucumbers. Sprinkle with the sesame seeds.
9. Serve warm or at room temperature.

Each serving provides:
473 Calories
10 g Fat
2 g Saturated Fat
73 mg Cholesterol
57 g Carbohydrate
37 g Protein
243 mg Sodium

Pork Lo Mein with Red Cabbage, Green Peas, and Bean Sprouts

Makes 4 to 6 servings

Lo mein is a Chinese noodle concoction using practically any ingredient. This version, which uses pork, bean sprouts, cabbage, and peas, makes a satisfying main dish.

1 tablespoon low-sodium soy sauce
2 tablespoons rice vinegar
8 ounces lean boneless pork loin
8 ounces Chinese egg noodles or linguine

Seasonings
1 tablespoon minced fresh ginger
1 medium onion, chopped
1 tablespoon minced fresh green chili pepper

On Your Tray

- Canola oil spray
- Bowl of pork in marinade
- Bowl of seasonings
- Bowl of vegetables
- Bowl of sauce
- Cornstarch mixture
- Bowl of noodles

Vegetables
2 cups fresh bean sprouts, rinsed and drained
1 cup shredded red cabbage
1 cup fresh or frozen green peas (if using fresh peas, first boil until tender)

Sauce
2 cups low-sodium chicken broth
3 tablespoons low-sodium soy sauce
1 teaspoon sugar

Additional Ingredients
1 tablespoon cornstarch dissolved in 2 tablespoons cold water
Canola oil spray

Preparation

1. Combine the soy sauce and rice vinegar in a bowl.
2. Trim the pork of excess fat and cut into ½-inch cubes. Add the pork to the soy sauce mixture and let marinate for 20 to 30 minutes.
3. Bring water to a boil in a large pot. Add the noodles and cook until *al dente*. Drain and place in a bowl with ¼ cup water to prevent sticking.
4. Combine the seasoning ingredients in a bowl.
5. Combine the vegetables in a bowl.
6. Combine the sauce ingredients in a bowl.
7. Assemble your cooking tray.

Cooking

1. Heat a nonstick wok over high heat for 2 minutes.
2. Carefully spray the wok with the canola oil spray. (If you have a gas stove, turn off the burner before you spray the wok.)
3. Add the pork and marinade and stir-fry for 2 minutes. Remove the pork from the wok and set aside in a bowl.
4. Rinse out the wok, then reheat it for 30 seconds. Respray with canola oil spray. Add the seasonings and stir-fry for 30 seconds.
5. Add the vegetables and stir-fry for 1 minute.
6. Add the sauce and bring to a boil. Cover, lower heat, and cook for 3 minutes.
7. Remove the cover, return the heat to high, add the pork to the wok, and stir to heat through.
8. Add the cornstarch mixture and stir until the sauce is thickened.
9. Add the noodles, and stir to heat through, about 2 minutes.
10. Remove from the wok and serve.

■

Each serving provides:
289 Calories
5 g Fat
2 g Saturated Fat
48 mg Cholesterol
37 g Carbohydrate
24 g Protein
505 mg Sodium

■

Turkey Wontons with Spicy Scallion Sauce

Makes about 36 wontons, serving 4 to 6

This dish makes an exotic pasta entrée. The wontons by themselves can be used in Wonton Soup (see index).

On Your Tray

- Canola oil spray
- Bowl of seasonings
- Bowl of vegetables
- Bowl of turkey mixture

Seasonings

- 1 tablespoon minced fresh ginger
- 1 tablespoon minced fresh garlic
- 1/2 cup finely minced onion
- 1/2 cup finely minced celery

Vegetables

- 1/2 cup finely chopped fresh mushrooms
- 1/4 cup finely chopped water chestnuts

Turkey Mixture

- 8 ounces lean ground turkey
- 2 tablespoons chopped scallion, both white and green parts
- 1 egg white, lightly beaten
- 1 tablespoon low-sodium soy sauce
- 1 tablespoon cornstarch

Additional Ingredients

- Canola oil spray
- 36 ready-made wonton wrappers (see note)
- Spicy Scallion Sauce (recipe follows)

Preparing the Filling

1. Combine the seasoning ingredients in a small bowl.
2. Combine the mushrooms and the water chestnuts in another small bowl.
3. Combine the turkey mixture ingredients in a bowl.
4. Assemble your cooking tray.

Cooking the Filling

1. Heat a nonstick wok over high heat for 2 minutes.
2. Carefully spray the wok with the canola oil spray. (If you have a gas stove, turn off the burner before you spray the wok.)
3. Add the seasonings and stir-fry for 30 seconds.
4. Add the mushrooms and water chestnuts and stir-fry for 1 minute. Remove from the wok and set aside to cool slightly, about 10 minutes.
5. Add the wok mixture to the uncooked turkey mixture and combine well.

Assembly

1. Working one at a time, place a wonton wrapper on your work surface and place a rounded teaspoon of the turkey filling in the center. (Keep the remaining wrappers covered with a slightly dampened towel so they don't dry out.)
2. Using your fingers, dampen the outer edge of the wonton with cold water and fold the wrapper in half, covering the filling and forming a triangle. Pinch the edges together to seal.
3. Bring the two wings of the triangle together, overlap them, moisten with a little cold water, and pinch to seal.

Cooking the Wontons

1. Bring several quarts of water to a boil in a large stockpot.
2. Carefully drop the wontons into the boiling water. Do not overcrowd; boil them in two separate batches if necessary.
3. Boil for about 6 minutes. The wontons will rise to the surface of the water when done. Drain and serve with the spicy scallion sauce.

NOTE Wonton wrappers are available in most well-stocked supermarkets.

Each serving (with sauce) provides:
210 Calories
2 g Fat
0.3 g Saturated Fat
24 mg Cholesterol
12 g Carbohydrate
11 g Protein
387 mg Sodium

■ Spicy Scallion Sauce

Makes 3 cups, serving 6

On Your Tray

- Canola oil spray
- Bowl of seasonings
- Bowl of red pepper
- Bowl of scallions
- Bowl of sauce
- Cornstarch mixture
- Coriander

Seasonings

1 tablespoon minced fresh ginger
1 tablespoon minced fresh garlic
1 tablespoon minced fresh green chili pepper
1/4 cup chopped onion

Vegetables

1/2 medium red bell pepper, seeds and ribs
    removed, chopped
6 scallions, both white and green parts, chopped

Sauce

3 cups low-sodium chicken broth
2 tablespoons low-sodium soy sauce
1 tablespoon dry sherry

Additional Ingredients

2 tablespoons cornstarch dissolved in 3 tablespoons
    cold water
2 tablespoons minced fresh coriander leaves or parsley
    for garnish
Canola oil spray

Preparation

1. Combine the seasoning ingredients in a small bowl.
2. Place the red pepper and the scallions in separate bowls.
3. Combine the sauce ingredients in a bowl.
4. Assemble your cooking tray.

Cooking

1. Heat a nonstick wok over high heat for 2 minutes.
2. Carefully spray the wok with the canola oil spray. (If you have a gas stove, turn off the burner before you spray the wok.) Add the seasonings and stir-fry for 30 seconds.
3. Add the red pepper and stir-fry for 30 seconds.
4. Add the scallions and stir-fry for 30 seconds.
5. Pour in the sauce and bring to a boil.
6. Stir in the cornstarch mixture and reduce heat to medium. Cook sauce for 3 minutes at a very low boil, stirring occasionally.
7. Remove from the wok and sprinkle with coriander.
8. Serve over noodles or turkey wontons.

■ ANTS CLIMBING A TREE

Makes 6 servings

Perhaps you have the imagination, as did the creators of this popular Chinese dish, to picture bits of ground meat among the noodles as ants climbing a tree. If that is not an appealing image to you, think of this instead as a hearty Szechuan noodle stir-fry. In this lowfat version, we substitute ground turkey for the traditional ground beef.

ON YOUR TRAY

- Canola oil spray
- Bowl of seasonings
- Bowl of turkey mixture
- Bowl of peppers
- Bowl of sauce
- Bowl of noodles
- Scallions

Turkey Mixture

- 8 ounces lean ground turkey
- 1/4 cup grated carrot
- 2 tablespoons finely chopped scallions
- 2 tablespoons finely chopped water chestnuts
- 2 tablespoons finely chopped fresh green chili peppers
- 1 tablespoon low-sodium soy sauce
- 2 teaspoons sesame oil

Noodles

- 8 ounces Chinese cellophane noodles

Seasonings

- 1 teaspoon minced fresh garlic
- 1 tablespoon minced fresh ginger

Vegetables

- 1 small red bell pepper, seeds and ribs removed, cut into 1-inch squares
- 1 small green bell pepper, seeds and ribs removed, cut into 1-inch squares

Sauce

- 1/2 cup low-sodium chicken broth
- 1 tablespoon rice vinegar
- 2 teaspoons low-sodium soy sauce

Additional Ingredients

- 1 cup thinly sliced scallions, both white and green parts, for garnish
- Canola oil spray

Preparation

1. Combine the turkey mixture ingredients in a large bowl.
2. Place the noodles in a large bowl and cover with boiling water. Set aside for 10 minutes, then drain. Rinse in cold water, drain well, and place in a bowl.
3. Combine the seasoning ingredients in a small bowl.
4. Combine the red and green peppers in a bowl.
5. Combine the sauce ingredients in a small bowl.
6. Assemble your cooking tray.

Cooking

1. Heat a nonstick wok over high heat for 2 minutes.
2. Carefully coat the bottom of the wok with the canola oil spray. (If you have a gas stove, turn off the burner before you spray the wok.) Add the seasonings and stir-fry for 15 seconds.
3. Add the turkey mixture and stir-fry for 2 minutes.
4. Add the peppers and stir-fry for 1 minute.
5. Pour in the sauce and stir to combine.
6. Add the cellophane noodles and toss to mix well.
7. Remove from the wok and sprinkle with the scallions.

■

Each serving provides:
218 Calories
3 g Fat
0.6 g Saturated Fat
25 mg Cholesterol
34 g Carbohydrate
13 g Protein
146 mg Sodium

■

■ BABY CLAMS AND NOODLES IN BLACK BEAN SAUCE

Makes 4 to 6 servings

Clams in black bean sauce is a classic Cantonese dish. This variation uses noodles and chili paste.

8 ounces thin Chinese egg noodles, cooked and drained

Seasonings
1 tablespoon minced fresh ginger
1 tablespoon minced fresh garlic

ON YOUR TRAY

- Canola oil spray
- Bowl of seasonings
- Bowl of onion
- Bowl of carrots
- Bowl of celery
- Bowl of mushrooms
- Bowl of clams
- Bowl of sauce
- Bowl of noodles

Vegetables and Clams
1/2 cup chopped onion
1 cup chopped celery
2 carrots, cut into 1/2-inch cubes
2 cups sliced fresh mushrooms
2 cans (10 ounces each) shelled whole baby clams, drained, juice reserved

Sauce
1 1/2 to 2 cups low-sodium chicken or vegetable broth
Reserved clam juice
1 tablespoon black bean sauce
2 teaspoons chili paste

Additional Ingredients
1 tablespoon cornstarch dissolved in 2 tablespoons cold water
3 scallions, both white and green parts, chopped for garnish
Canola oil spray

Preparation

1. Place the noodles in a bowl with ¼ cup of cold water to prevent them from sticking.
2. Combine the seasoning ingredients in a small bowl.
3. Place the onion, celery, carrots, mushrooms, and clams in separate bowls.
4. Combine the sauce ingredients in a bowl.
5. Assemble your cooking tray.

Cooking

1. Heat a nonstick wok over high heat for 2 minutes.
2. Carefully spray the wok with the canola oil spray. (If you have a gas stove, turn off the burner before you spray the wok.) Add the seasonings and stir-fry for 15 seconds.
3. Add the onion and stir-fry for 30 seconds.
4. Add the carrots and celery and stir-fry for 2 minutes.
5. Add the mushrooms and stir-fry for 1 minute.
6. Add the clams and the sauce and bring to a boil.
7. Add the noodles. Toss to mix well with the sauce. Cover and cook for 3 minutes.
8. Add the cornstarch mixture, if necessary, to thicken the sauce and cook for 1 minute more.
9. Remove from the wok. Sprinkle with the scallions and serve.

■
Each serving provides:
227 Calories
2 g Fat
0.2 g Saturated Fat
43 mg Cholesterol
38 g Carbohydrate
15 g Protein
418 mg Sodium
■

■ LAND AND SEA NOODLES

Makes 4 to 6 servings

This Chinese one-dish meal has it all—shrimp, chicken, noodles, and vegetables.

8 ounces thin Chinese egg noodles, cooked and drained

Marinade
1 egg white, lightly beaten
2 teaspoons dry sherry
2 teaspoons cornstarch

Shrimp and Chicken
6 ounces fresh small shrimp, peeled and deveined
1 skinless and boneless chicken breast (about 6 ounces), cut into 3/4-inch pieces

ON YOUR TRAY

- Canola oil spray
- Bowl of marinated chicken
- Bowl of marinated shrimp
- Bowl of seasonings
- Bowl of vegetables
- Bowl of sauce
- Bowl of noodles
- Scallions

Seasonings
1 teaspoon minced fresh ginger
1 teaspoon minced fresh garlic
1 cup finely chopped onion

Vegetables
3 ounces fresh green beans, cut into slivers 2 inches long
1 cup small cauliflower florets
1 cucumber, peeled, cut in half lengthwise, seeds removed, and cut into thin slices

Sauce
1 cup low-sodium chicken broth
2 tablespoons low-sodium soy sauce
1 tablespoon dry sherry

Additional Ingredients
1 cup thinly sliced scallions, both white and green parts, for garnish
Canola oil spray

Preparation

1. Place the noodles in a bowl with ¼ cup of cold water to prevent them from sticking.
2. Combine the marinade ingredients in a small bowl and mix until smooth. Divide the marinade into two bowls.
3. Add the shrimp to one bowl of the marinade and the chicken to the other. Set both aside for 20 to 30 minutes.
4. Combine the seasoning ingredients in a small bowl.
5. Combine the vegetables in a bowl.
6. Combine the sauce ingredients in a small bowl.
7. Assemble your cooking tray.

Cooking

1. Heat a nonstick wok over high heat for 2 minutes.
2. Carefully spray the wok with the canola oil spray. (If you have a gas stove, turn off the burner before you spray the wok.) Add the chicken and stir-fry for 1 minute.
3. Add the shrimp and stir-fry for 30 seconds.
4. Remove the chicken and shrimp from the wok and set aside.
5. Rinse out the wok, then reheat it for 30 seconds. Respray with canola oil spray. Add the seasonings and stir-fry for 30 seconds.
6. Add the vegetables and stir-fry for 30 seconds.
7. Add the sauce, cover, reduce the heat to medium and cook for 3 minutes.
8. Remove the cover, add the noodles, and stir to heat through, about 2 minutes.
9. Return the shrimp and chicken to the wok and stir to mix.
10. Remove from the wok, sprinkle with the scallions, and serve.

> ■
> Each serving provides:
> 237 Calories
> 3 g Fat
> 1 g Saturated Fat
> 47 mg Cholesterol
> 35 g Carbohydrate
> 18 g Protein
> 207 mg Sodium
> ■

Triple Mushroom Rice Noodles with Turkey

Makes 4 to 6 servings

This is a mildly spicy vegetable-noodle stir-fry with just enough turkey to be noticed. It can be made into a vegetarian dish by leaving out the turkey and substituting vegetable broth for the chicken broth. You can adjust the spiciness by increasing or decreasing the amount of chilies.

8 ounces skinless and boneless fresh turkey cut into
¼ × 2-inch strips
1 tablespoon low-sodium soy sauce
8 ounces rice noodles

On Your Tray

- Canola oil spray
- Bowl of marinated turkey
- Bowl of seasonings
- Bowl of fresh mushrooms
- Bowl of bean sprouts
- Bowl of julienned scallions
- Bowl of Chinese and straw mushrooms and baby corn
- Bowl of noodles
- Bowl of sauce
- Bowl of peas
- Chopped scallions

Seasonings
1 tablespoon minced fresh ginger
1 tablespoon minced fresh garlic
2 teaspoons minced fresh green chili peppers
1 cup finely chopped onion

Vegetables
½ cup dried Chinese mushrooms, soaked in hot water for
30 minutes
½ cup drained canned straw mushrooms
8 ears baby corn, drained and cut in half lengthwise
2 cups sliced fresh mushrooms
2 cups bean sprouts, rinsed and drained
6 scallions, both white and green parts, cut into
⅛ × 2-inch julienne
1 cup frozen green peas, thawed

Sauce
1 cup low-sodium chicken broth
2 tablespoons low-sodium soy sauce
1 tablespoon hoisin sauce
1 tablespoon dry sherry
2 teaspoons sesame oil

Additional Ingredients

3 scallions, both white and green parts, chopped
for garnish
Canola oil spray

Preparation

1. Combine the turkey and soy sauce in a bowl and set aside for 20 to 30 minutes.
2. Bring 3 quarts of water to a boil, add the noodles, and separate with a fork. Return the water to a boil and cook the noodles for 3 minutes. Remove the pan from the heat and leave the noodles in the hot water for 15 minutes. Drain and set aside.
3. Combine the seasoning ingredients in a small bowl.
4. Rinse the Chinese mushrooms and remove and discard the tough stems. Cut the caps into 1/8-inch strips and place in a bowl.
5. Add the straw mushrooms and baby corn to the Chinese mushroom strips.
6. Place the fresh mushrooms, bean sprouts, julienned scallions, and green peas in separate bowls.
7. Combine the sauce ingredients in a small bowl.
8. Assemble your cooking tray.

Cooking

1. Heat a nonstick wok over high heat for 2 minutes.
2. Carefully spray the wok with the canola oil spray. (If you have a gas stove, turn off the burner before you spray the wok.) Add the marinated turkey. Stir-fry for 1 minute, remove from the wok, and set aside.
3. Rinse out the wok, then reheat it for 30 seconds. Respray with canola oil spray. Add the seasonings and fresh mushrooms and stir-fry for 1 minute.

(continues)

RICE AND NOODLES

4. Add the bean sprouts and stir-fry for 30 seconds.
5. Add the julienned scallions and stir-fry for 30 seconds.
6. Add the Chinese mushrooms, straw mushrooms, and baby corn and stir-fry for 30 seconds.
7. Add the noodles and the sauce and stir-fry for 1 minute, tossing well to combine.
8. Add the cooked turkey and the peas and stir-fry for 30 seconds.
9. Remove from the wok to a serving bowl. Garnish with the chopped scallions and serve.

■

Each serving provides:
320 Calories
4 g Fat
0.7 g Saturated Fat
30 mg Cholesterol
48 g Carbohydrate
19 g Protein
279 mg Sodium

■

RICE AND NOODLES

EIGHT

FISH AND SEAFOOD

STIR-FRIED BAY SCALLOPS WITH FRESH ASPARAGUS

BAY SCALLOPS WITH CUCUMBER

SEA SCALLOPS WITH BLACK BEAN SAUCE

SEA SCALLOPS WITH SHIITAKE MUSHROOMS

SZECHUAN SHRIMP

JUMBO SHRIMP WITH LEMON-GINGER SAUCE

KUNG PAO SHRIMP

ALASKAN KING CRAB WITH SNOW PEAS AND WATER CHESTNUTS

CRAB FU YUNG OMELET

OYSTERS IN GINGER-SCALLION SAUCE

MUSSELS IN SPICY ORANGE SAUCE

SEARED HOT AND PUNGENT SWORDFISH STEAK

STIR-FRIED SALMON WITH ASPARAGUS AND BABY CORN

BAKED TUNA WITH CITRUS-GINGER SAUCE

FIVE-SPICE TUNA STEAK

SPINACH-STUFFED FLOUNDER

GRILLED FISH KABOBS WITH ANISE

MAHIMAHI WITH MANGO AND PINEAPPLE

BAKED COD WITH CHINESE CABBAGE

■ STIR-FRIED BAY SCALLOPS WITH FRESH ASPARAGUS

Makes 3 to 4 servings

Tiny bay scallops are very delicate. They can be ruined by overcooking, so be sure to follow the suggested cooking times carefully.

1 pound bay scallops, rinsed in cold water and drained
2 tablespoons dry white wine or dry sherry

Seasonings
1/4 cup chopped scallions, both white and green parts
1 tablespoon minced fresh ginger
1 teaspoon minced fresh garlic

ON YOUR TRAY

- Canola oil spray
- Bowl of scallops in marinade
- Bowl of seasonings
- Bowl of asparagus and yellow pepper
- Bowl of sauce
- Cornstarch mixture

Vegetables
8 ounces fresh asparagus, trimmed and cut into 1-inch pieces
1 medium yellow bell pepper, seeds and ribs removed, and coarsely chopped

Sauce
1 cup dry white wine
1 tablespoon oyster sauce
1 tablespoon fresh lemon juice
1 teaspoon minced fresh lemon peel

Additional Ingredients
1 teaspoon cornstarch dissolved in 1 tablespoon cold water
Canola oil spray

■

Each serving provides:
201 Calories
1.4 g Fat
0.2 g Saturated Fat
38 mg Cholesterol
14 g Carbohydrate
23 g Protein
213 mg Sodium

■

Preparation

1. Put the scallops in a bowl with 2 tablespoons wine and let marinate for 20 to 30 minutes.
2. Combine the seasoning ingredients in a bowl.

3. Combine the asparagus and the yellow pepper in a bowl.
4. Combine the sauce ingredients in a bowl.
5. Assemble your cooking tray.

Cooking

1. Heat a nonstick wok over high heat for 2 minutes.
2. Carefully spray the wok with the canola oil spray. (If you have a gas stove, turn off the burner before you spray the wok.) Add the scallops and marinade and stir-fry for 30 seconds. Remove the scallops from the wok and set aside.
3. Rinse out the wok, then reheat it for 30 seconds. Respray the wok with canola oil spray. Add the seasonings and stir-fry for 30 seconds.
4. Add the asparagus and yellow pepper and stir-fry for 1 minute.
5. Add the sauce and bring to a boil. Cover and simmer for 3 minutes.
6. Remove the cover, return the scallops to the wok, and stir to heat through.
7. Stir in the cornstarch mixture and cook until sauce is thickened, about 30 seconds.
8. Remove from the wok and serve.

■ BAY SCALLOPS WITH CUCUMBER

Makes 4 servings

1 egg white, lightly beaten
1 tablespoon cornstarch dissolved in 2 tablespoons
   cold water
1 pound bay scallops, rinsed in cold water and drained

Seasonings
1 tablespoon minced fresh garlic
1 tablespoon minced fresh ginger

ON YOUR TRAY

- Canola oil spray
- Bowl of scallops in marinade
- Bowl of seasonings
- Bowl of cucumber and red pepper
- Bowl of sauce
- Parsley

Vegetables
1 large cucumber, peeled, cut in half lengthwise, seeded, and cut into 1/8-inch slices
$1/2$ medium red bell pepper, seeds and ribs removed, and cut into $1/4$-inch squares

Sauce
$1/2$ cup low-sodium chicken or vegetable broth
1 tablespoon fresh lemon juice
1 tablespoon low-sodium soy sauce
1 teaspoon cornstarch

Additional Ingredients
2 tablespoons chopped fresh parsley for garnish
   Canola oil spray

Preparation

1. Combine the egg white and cornstarch mixture in a bowl and stir until smooth.
2. Add the scallops to the bowl and let marinate for 20 to 30 minutes.
3. Combine the seasoning ingredients in a small bowl.

4. Combine the cucumber and the red pepper in a bowl.
5. Combine the sauce ingredients in a small bowl and stir well until the cornstarch is dissolved.
6. Assemble your cooking tray.

Cooking

1. Heat a nonstick wok over high heat for 2 minutes.
2. Carefully spray the wok with the canola oil spray. (If you have a gas stove, turn off the burner before you spray the wok.) Add the bay scallops and stir-fry for 30 seconds. Remove the scallops from the wok and set aside in a bowl.
3. Rinse out the wok, then reheat it for 30 seconds. Respray the wok with canola oil spray. Add the seasonings and stir-fry for 15 seconds.
4. Add the cucumber and red pepper and stir-fry for 1 minute.
5. Add the sauce and bring to a boil to thicken a little.
6. Return the bay scallops to the wok and stir just to heat through, about 30 seconds.
7. Transfer to a serving platter and sprinkle with the parsley.

Each serving provides:
144 Calories
2 g Fat
0.1 g Saturated Fat
58 mg Cholesterol
12 g Carbohydrate
26 g Protein
301 mg Sodium

■ Sea Scallops with Black Bean Sauce

Makes 3 to 4 servings

12 ounces sea scallops (about 18), rinsed in cold water
and drained
1 tablespoon minced fresh garlic
2 cups fresh snow peas (about 6 ounces), stems and
strings removed
8 ounces fresh bean sprouts, rinsed and drained

On Your Tray

- Canola oil spray
- Bowl of garlic
- Bowl of snow peas
- Bowl of bean sprouts
- Bowl of sauce
- Cornstarch mixture
- Bowl of scallops

Sauce

1/2 cup low-sodium vegetable or chicken broth
1 tablespoon black bean sauce
1 tablespoon low-sodium soy sauce
1 tablespoon ketchup

Additional Ingredients

2 teaspoons cornstarch dissolved in 1 tablespoon
cold water
Canola oil spray

Preparation

1. Place the scallops, garlic, snow peas, and bean
sprouts in separate bowls.
2. Combine the sauce ingredients in a small bowl.
3. Assemble your cooking tray.

Cooking

1. Heat a nonstick wok over high heat for 2 minutes.
2. Carefully spray the wok with the canola oil spray.
(If you have a gas stove, turn off the burner before
you spray the wok.) Add the garlic and stir-fry for
15 seconds.

■
Each serving provides:
157 Calories
1 g Fat
0 g Saturated Fat
45 mg Cholesterol
18 g Carbohydrate
26 g Protein
498 mg Sodium
■

3. Add the snow peas and stir-fry for 30 seconds.
4. Add the bean sprouts and stir-fry for 30 seconds.
5. Add the sauce, stir in the cornstarch mixture, and cook to thicken, about 30 seconds.
6. Add the scallops and stir, cooking until the scallops are opaque, about 2 minutes.
7. Remove from the wok and serve.

■ Sea Scallops with Shiitake Mushrooms

Makes 3 to 4 servings

1 tablespoon dry sherry
1 tablespoon low-sodium soy sauce
8 ounces sea scallops (12 to 14), rinsed in cold water
  and drained

Seasonings
1 cup finely chopped onion
1 tablespoon minced fresh garlic
1 teaspoon minced fresh ginger

On Your Tray

- Canola oil spray
- Bowl of scallops in marinade
- Bowl of seasonings
- Bowl of mushrooms, zucchini, and parsley
- Oyster sauce
- Chives

Additional Ingredients
4 ounces fresh shiitake mushrooms, rinsed (about 1 cup)
2 small green zucchini, cut into 1/8-inch-thick rounds
1/4 cup chopped fresh parsley
3 tablespoons oyster sauce
1 tablespoon chopped fresh chives for garnish
  Canola oil spray

Preparation

1. Combine the sherry and the soy sauce in a bowl.
2. Add the scallops to the bowl and let marinate for 20 to 30 minutes.
3. Combine the seasoning ingredients in a small bowl.
4. Remove and discard the shiitake mushroom stems. Cut the caps into quarters.
5. Combine the mushrooms, zucchini, and parsley in a bowl.
6. Assemble your cooking tray.

Cooking

1. Heat a nonstick wok over high heat for 2 minutes.
2. Carefully spray the wok with the canola oil spray. (If you have a gas stove, turn off the burner before you spray the wok.) Add the scallops and their marinade and stir-fry for 30 seconds. Remove from the wok and set aside.
3. Rinse out the wok, then reheat it for 30 seconds. Respray the wok with canola oil spray. Add the seasonings and stir-fry for 30 seconds.
4. Add the mushrooms, zucchini, and parsley and stir-fry for 1 minute.
5. Add the oyster sauce and stir-fry for 30 seconds.
6. Return the scallops to the wok and stir to heat through, about 15 seconds.
7. Remove from the wok and sprinkle with the chives.

Each serving provides:
110 Calories
0.8 g Fat
0.1 g Saturated Fat
29 mg Cholesterol
15 g Carbohydrate
12 g Protein
258 mg Sodium

■ SZECHUAN SHRIMP

Makes 6 servings

Even though this is a Szechuan dish, it is only mildly spicy because no chili peppers are used.

1 egg white, lightly beaten
2 teaspoons cornstarch
2 teaspoons low-sodium soy sauce
1 pound jumbo shrimp (about 18), peeled and deveined

Seasonings
1 tablespoon minced fresh garlic
1 teaspoon minced fresh ginger
2 scallions, both white and green parts, chopped

ON YOUR TRAY

- Canola oil spray
- Bowl of shrimp in marinade
- Bowl of seasonings
- Bowl of vegetables
- Bowl of sauce

Vegetables
2 cups fresh snow peas (about 6 ounces), stems and strings removed, cut in half on the diagonal
1/2 cup drained canned water chestnuts, rinsed and coarsely chopped
4 scallions, both white and green parts, chopped

Sauce
1/2 cup low-sodium chicken or vegetable broth
1 tablespoon rice vinegar
1 tablespoon sugar
2 tablespoons ketchup
1 tablespoon sesame oil
1 tablespoon chili paste

Additional Ingredient
Canola oil spray

FISH AND SEAFOOD

Preparation

1. Combine the egg white, cornstarch, and soy sauce in a bowl. Stir until the cornstarch is dissolved.
2. Add the shrimp to the bowl and let marinate for 20 to 30 minutes.
3. Combine the seasoning ingredients in a small bowl.
4. Combine the vegetables in a small bowl.
5. Combine the sauce ingredients in another small bowl.
6. Assemble your cooking tray.

Cooking

1. Heat a nonstick wok over high heat for 2 minutes.
2. Carefully spray the wok with the canola oil spray. (If you have a gas stove, turn off the burner before you spray the wok.)
3. Add the shrimp and marinade and stir-fry for 1 minute. Remove the shrimp from the wok and set aside in a bowl.
4. Rinse out the wok, then reheat it for 30 seconds. Respray the wok with canola oil spray. Add the seasonings and stir-fry for 15 seconds.
5. Add the vegetables and stir-fry for 1 minute.
6. Add the sauce and bring to a boil.
7. Return the shrimp to the wok and stir for 1 minute to heat through.
8. Remove from the wok and serve.

■

Each serving provides:
143 Calories
4 g Fat
0.6 g Saturated Fat
116 mg Cholesterol
12 g Carbohydrate
18 g Protein
357 mg Sodium

■

JUMBO SHRIMP WITH LEMON-GINGER SAUCE

Makes 2 to 3 servings

1 teaspoon low-sodium soy sauce

1 teaspoon dry sherry

8 ounces jumbo shrimp (about 9), peeled, deveined, and butterflied (see note)

Seasonings

1/4 cup finely chopped onion

1 teaspoon minced fresh garlic

1 teaspoon minced fresh ginger

ON YOUR TRAY

- Canola oil spray
- Bowl of shrimp in marinade
- Bowl of seasonings
- Bowl of green pepper
- Bowl of mushrooms
- Bowl of snow peas
- Bowl of scallions
- Bowl of sauce
- Cornstarch mixture
- Lemon zest

Vegetables

1/2 cup slivered green bell pepper

1 cup sliced fresh mushrooms

1 cup snow peas (about 3 ounces), stems and strings removed

1/2 cup sliced scallions, both white and green parts

Sauce

1/4 cup low-sodium chicken or vegetable broth

1/4 cup fresh lemon juice (1 large lemon)

1 1/2 tablespoons sugar

1 tablespoon minced fresh ginger

Additional Ingredients

2 teaspoons cornstarch dissolved in 1 tablespoon cold water

1 tablespoon fresh lemon zest for garnish
Canola oil spray

Preparation

1. Combine the soy sauce and sherry in a bowl.
2. Add the shrimp to the bowl and let marinate for 20 minutes.
3. Combine the seasoning ingredients in a small bowl.
4. Place the green pepper, mushrooms, snow peas, and scallions in separate bowls.
5. Combine the sauce ingredients in a small bowl.
6. Assemble your cooking tray.

Cooking

1. Heat a nonstick wok over high heat for 2 minutes.
2. Carefully spray the wok with the canola oil spray. (If you have a gas stove, turn off the burner before you spray the wok.)
3. Add the shrimp and the marinade and stir-fry for 1 minute. Remove the shrimp from the wok and set aside in a bowl.
4. Rinse out the wok, then reheat it for 30 seconds. Respray the wok with canola oil spray. Add the seasonings and stir-fry for 15 seconds.
5. Add the green pepper and stir-fry for 30 seconds.
6. Add the mushrooms and stir-fry for 30 seconds.
7. Add the snow peas and scallions, stir-fry for 30 seconds, and add the sauce and stir.
8. Return the shrimp to the wok and stir to heat through, about 30 seconds. Add the cornstarch mixture, if necessary, to thicken the sauce.
9. Remove from the wok, sprinkle with lemon zest, and serve.

NOTE   To butterfly, make a 1-inch cut into the wide part of each shrimp and press to flatten slightly.

■

Each serving provides:
154 Calories
2 g Fat
0.3 g Saturated Fat
115 mg Cholesterol
20 g Carbohydrate
18 g Protein
167 mg Sodium

■

■ KUNG PAO SHRIMP

Makes 4 to 6 servings

Kung pao dishes—hot, spicy foods from Szechuan province—are popular restaurant entrées. If you prefer less spice, cut the quantity of chili peppers in half.

1 egg white, lightly beaten
1 tablespoon dry sherry
1 tablespoon cornstarch
1 pound jumbo shrimp (about 18), peeled and deveined

Seasonings

3 to 4 dried red chili peppers, 1 1/2 to 2 inches long
1 cup chopped scallion, both white and green parts
1 teaspoon minced fresh ginger
1 tablespoon minced fresh garlic

ON YOUR TRAY

- Canola oil spray
- Bowl of shrimp in marinade
- Bowl of seasonings
- Bowl of peppers and celery
- Bowl of scallions
- Bowl of sauce

Vegetables

1 red bell pepper, seeds and ribs removed, cut into thin slivers 2 inches long
1 green bell pepper, seeds and ribs removed, cut into thin slivers 2 inches long
2 stalks celery, cut on the diagonal into thin slivers 2 inches long
4 scallions, both white and green parts, cut into thin slivers 2 inches long

Sauce

1/4 cup water or low-sodium vegetable broth
2 tablespoons rice vinegar
1 tablespoon low-sodium soy sauce
1 tablespoon sugar

Additional Ingredient

Canola oil spray

Preparation

1. Combine the egg white, sherry, and cornstarch in a small bowl and mix until the cornstarch is dissolved.
2. Add the shrimp to the bowl and let marinate for 20 to 30 minutes.
3. Combine the seasoning ingredients in a small bowl.
4. Combine the red and green peppers and celery in a bowl. Place the slivered scallions in a separate bowl.
5. Combine the sauce ingredients in a bowl.
6. Assemble your cooking tray.

Cooking

1. Heat a nonstick wok over high heat for 2 minutes.
2. Carefully spray the wok with the canola oil spray. (If you have a gas stove, turn off the burner before you spray the wok.) Add the shrimp and marinade and stir-fry for 1 minute. Remove the shrimp to a bowl and set aside.
3. Rinse out the wok, then reheat it for 30 seconds. Respray the wok with canola oil spray. Add the seasonings and stir-fry for 15 seconds.
4. Add the peppers and celery and stir-fry for 1 minute.
5. Add the scallions and stir-fry for 30 seconds.
6. Stir in the sauce and bring to a boil.
7. Return the shrimp to the wok and stir-fry until heated through, about 1 minute. Remove from the wok. Before serving, take out the chili peppers and discard them.

■

Each serving provides:
108 Calories
2 g Fat
0.3 g Saturated Fat
115 mg Cholesterol
9 g Carbohydrate
17 g Protein
213 mg Sodium

■

ALASKAN KING CRAB WITH SNOW PEAS AND WATER CHESTNUTS

Makes 6 servings

Fresh water chestnuts have a sweeter, more distinctive taste than canned. If you find fresh water chestnuts (in the refrigerated produce section of your market), try them in this recipe.

- 1 tablespoon low-sodium soy sauce
- 1 tablespoon rice vinegar
- 1/4 teaspoon five-spice powder
- 4 pounds cooked king crab legs, in shell

Seasonings

- 1 tablespoon minced fresh garlic
- 1 teaspoon minced fresh ginger

ON YOUR TRAY

- Canola oil spray
- Bowl of seasonings
- Bowl of snow peas and water chestnuts
- Bowl of crabmeat in marinade
- Bowl of sauce
- Cornstarch mixture

Vegetables

- 6 ounces fresh snow peas (about 2 cups), stems and strings removed
- 6 ounces fresh water chestnuts, peeled and sliced, or 1 can (8 ounces), drained

Sauce

- 3/4 cup low-sodium vegetable or chicken broth
- 1/4 cup dry white wine
- 1 tablespoon low-sodium soy sauce

Additional Ingredients

- 1 tablespoon cornstarch dissolved in 2 tablespoons cold water
- Canola oil spray

Preparation

1. Combine the soy sauce, rice vinegar, and five-spice powder in a bowl.
2. Remove the long pieces of crabmeat from the shells and cut into 1-inch lengths. Add to the soy sauce mixture and let marinate for 20 to 30 minutes.
3. Combine the seasoning ingredients in a small bowl.
4. Combine the snow peas and water chestnuts in a bowl.
5. Combine the sauce ingredients in a small bowl.
6. Assemble your cooking tray.

Cooking

1. Heat a nonstick wok over high heat for 2 minutes.
2. Carefully spray the wok with the canola oil spray. (If you have a gas stove, turn off the burner before you spray the wok.) Add the seasonings and stir-fry for 15 seconds.
3. Add the snow peas and water chestnuts and stir-fry for 2 minutes.
4. Add the crabmeat and marinade, stir in the sauce, and bring to a boil.
5. Add the cornstarch mixture and stir about 1 minute, or until the sauce is thickened.
6. Remove from the wok and serve.

Each serving provides:
75 Calories
1 g Fat
0.1 g Saturated Fat
42 mg Cholesterol
8 g Carbohydrate
9 g Protein
223 mg Sodium

■ CRAB FU YUNG OMELET

Makes 10 to 12 omelets, serving 6 to 8

Egg fu yung is the Chinese version of an omelet. It is normally made with whole eggs, but we use egg substitute to cut down on cholesterol. We think the results are still good. If you wish, substitute shrimp or leftover cooked chicken, turkey, or pork for the crabmeat.

1 1/2	cups liquid egg substitute
1	tablespoon low-sodium soy sauce
1	tablespoon dry sherry
1	tablespoon minced fresh ginger
1	teaspoon minced fresh garlic
1/2	teaspoon white pepper
1	cup flaked crabmeat
1	cup finely chopped green cabbage
1	cup fresh bean sprouts, rinsed, drained, and coarsely chopped
1/4	cup finely chopped onion
1/4	cup finely chopped green bell pepper
1/4	cup chopped scallions, both white and green parts
3	tablespoons chopped fresh parsley
	Canola oil spray

1. Combine the egg substitute, soy sauce, sherry, ginger, garlic, and white pepper in a large mixing bowl.
2. Add the remaining ingredients except canola oil spray to the egg substitute mixture and stir well.
3. Heat a nonstick skillet or griddle over medium heat.
4. Carefully spray the skillet with the canola oil spray. (If you have a gas stove, turn off the burner before you spray the skillet.)

■

Each serving provides:
107 Calories
0.6 g Fat
0.1 g Saturated Fat
34 mg Cholesterol
9 g Carbohydrate
15 g Protein
301 mg Sodium

■

FISH AND SEAFOOD

5. Using a half-cup measure, spoon mounds of the egg substitute mixture on the skillet (3 or 4 at a time, as you would pancakes) and cook about 2 minutes. Carefully turn over the omelets and cook for 1 additional minute.

6. Transfer the omelets to a heatproof platter and keep warm in a low oven (200°). Continue making omelets until all the egg substitute mixture is used. You may want to wash the skillet after two batches, and respray it with canola oil spray before cooking the remaining omelets.

OYSTERS IN GINGER-SCALLION SAUCE

Makes 4 servings

1 cup shucked oysters with their juice

Seasonings
1 cup chopped onion
1 teaspoon minced fresh ginger

ON YOUR TRAY

- Canola oil spray
- Bowl of seasonings
- Bowl of celery
- Bowl of red pepper
- Bowl of scallions
- Bowl of oysters with juices
- Oyster sauce
- Parsley

Vegetables
2 stalks celery, thinly sliced on the diagonal into 2-inch slivers
1 medium red bell pepper, seeds and ribs removed, cut into 2-inch slivers
6 scallions, both white and green parts, cut into 2-inch slivers

Additional Ingredients
2 tablespoons oyster sauce
1 tablespoon chopped fresh parsley for garnish
Canola oil spray

Preparation

1. If the oysters are large, cut them into 2 or 3 pieces. Place in a bowl with their juices.
2. Combine the seasoning ingredients in a small bowl.
3. Place the celery, red pepper, and scallions in separate bowls.
4. Assemble your cooking tray.

Cooking

1. Heat a nonstick wok over high heat for 2 minutes.
2. Carefully spray the wok with the canola oil spray. (If you have a gas stove, turn off the burner before you spray the wok.) Add the seasonings and stir-fry for 15 seconds.
3. Add the celery and stir-fry for 1 minute.
4. Add the red pepper and stir-fry for 1 minute.
5. Add the scallions and stir-fry for 30 seconds.
6. Add the oysters and their juices and stir-fry for 30 seconds.
7. Add the oyster sauce and stir-fry for 30 seconds.
8. Remove from the wok. Sprinkle with the parsley and serve.

Each serving provides:
84 Calories
2 g Fat
0.4 g Saturated Fat
29 mg Cholesterol
13 g Carbohydrate
6 g Protein
131 mg Sodium

■ MUSSELS IN SPICY ORANGE SAUCE

Makes 3 to 4 servings

You wouldn't expect to find either frozen orange juice concentrate or mussels in traditional Chinese recipes. But they make an appealing combination with garlic, ginger, and chili paste in this contemporary variation. If you prefer, substitute little neck clams for the mussels.

ON YOUR TRAY

- Canola oil spray
- Bowl of seasonings
- Bowl of sauce
- Bowl of mussels
- Scallions

Seasonings

1/2 cup finely chopped onion

1 tablespoon minced fresh garlic

1 tablespoon minced fresh ginger

Sauce

1/2 cup low-sodium chicken or vegetable broth

1/2 cup dry white wine

1 tablespoon frozen orange juice concentrate

1 teaspoon chili paste

Seafood

36 fresh mussels in the shell

Additional Ingredients

2 tablespoons chopped scallions for garnish

Canola oil spray

Preparation

1. Combine the seasoning ingredients in a small bowl.
2. Combine the sauce ingredients in another small bowl.
3. Scrub the mussels well. If you find any strands of fibers attached to the shells, pull them off. (These are called "beards.") Place the mussels in a large bowl.
4. Assemble your cooking tray.

■

Each serving provides:
240 Calories
3 g Fat
0.3 g Saturated Fat
87 mg Cholesterol
14 g Carbohydrate
34 g Protein
214 mg Sodium

■

Cooking

1. Heat a nonstick wok over high heat for 2 minutes.
2. Carefully spray the wok with the canola oil spray. (If you have a gas stove, turn off the burner before you spray the wok.) Add the seasonings and stir-fry for 15 seconds.
3. Pour in the sauce, cover, reduce the heat to low and simmer for 3 minutes.
4. Turn the heat to high, add the mussels, cover again, and cook for 5 minutes.
5. Divide the mussels among individual serving bowls. Spoon the sauce over the mussels and garnish with the scallions.

■ Seared Hot and Pungent Swordfish Steak

Makes 4 servings

The swordfish is seared to char the outside and seal in the juices. The vegetables and pineapple are stir-fried to create the sauce for this exceptionally tasty seafood dish.

2 teaspoons low-sodium soy sauce

2 teaspoons dry sherry

2 swordfish steaks (about 8 ounces each), 1/2 inch thick

Seasonings

2 teaspoons minced fresh ginger

2 teaspoons minced fresh garlic

2 teaspoons minced fresh green chili peppers

On Your Tray

- Canola oil spray
- Marinated swordfish steaks
- Bowl of seasonings
- Bowl of cucumber
- Bowl of green pepper
- Bowl of pineapple
- Bowl of scallions
- Bowl of sauce
- Cornstarch mixture

Vegetables and Fruit

1 medium cucumber, peeled, cut in half lengthwise, seeded and cut into slivers

1 medium green bell pepper, seeds and ribs removed, and cut into slivers

2 cups fresh or canned pineapple chunks

1/2 cup chopped scallions, both white and green parts

Sauce

1/2 cup low-sodium vegetable or chicken broth

1/4 cup frozen pineapple juice concentrate

1 tablespoon low-sodium soy sauce

1 teaspoon chili paste

Additional Ingredients

1 teaspoon cornstarch dissolved in 2 teaspoons cold water

Canola oil spray

Preparation

1. Combine the soy sauce and sherry in a cup.
2. Rub the soy sauce mixture onto both sides of the swordfish steaks and let marinate for 30 minutes.
3. Combine the seasoning ingredients in a small bowl.
4. Place the cucumber, green pepper, pineapple, and scallions in separate bowls.
5. Combine the sauce ingredients in a bowl.
6. Assemble your cooking tray.

Cooking

1. Heat a nonstick wok over high heat for 2 minutes.
2. Carefully spray the wok with the canola oil spray. (If you have a gas stove, turn off the burner before you spray the wok.) Place 1 swordfish steak in the wok and sear the bottom over high heat for about 2 minutes. Turn and sear the other side until dark brown and slightly charred, about 2 minutes. Remove to a platter.
2. Rinse out the wok, then reheat it for 2 minutes. Respray the wok with canola oil spray. Repeat the process, searing the second swordfish steak. Remove to the platter and keep warm in a low oven.
4. Rinse out the wok again. Heat the wok over high heat for 2 minutes. Carefully spray the bottom with canola oil spray. Add the seasonings and stir-fry for 15 seconds.
5. Add the cucumber and green pepper and stir-fry for 30 seconds.
6. Add the pineapple and scallions and stir-fry for 30 seconds.
7. Give the sauce a stir and pour it into the wok. Stir-fry for 30 seconds. Add the cornstarch mixture, if necessary, to thicken the sauce.
8. Pour the sauce over the swordfish steaks and serve.

Each serving provides:
342 Calories
6 g Fat
2 g Saturated Fat
56 mg Cholesterol
50 g Carbohydrate
24 g Protein
340 mg Sodium

STIR-FRIED SALMON WITH ASPARAGUS AND BABY CORN

Makes 3 to 4 servings

The attractive combination of elegant ingredients in this dish makes it a delicious choice for a small dinner party.

1 tablespoon low-sodium soy sauce
1 tablespoon dry sherry
1 tablespoon rice vinegar
1 teaspoon cornstarch
12 ounces salmon fillet, skin and bones removed, and cut into 1-inch cubes

Seasonings

1 teaspoon minced fresh ginger
1/4 cup chopped scallions, both white and green parts

Vegetables

8 ounces fresh asparagus, trimmed and cut into 2-inch lengths
8 ears baby corn, drained and cut in half lengthwise

Sauce

1/2 cup low-sodium chicken or vegetable broth
1 tablespoon low-sodium soy sauce
1 tablespoon hoisin sauce

Additional Ingredients

Zest of 1 lemon for garnish
Canola oil spray

ON YOUR TRAY

- Canola oil spray
- Bowl of salmon in marinade
- Bowl of seasonings
- Bowl of asparagus
- Bowl of baby corn
- Bowl of sauce
- Lemon zest

Preparation

1. Combine the soy sauce, sherry, rice vinegar, and cornstarch in a small bowl and mix well until cornstarch is dissolved.
2. Add the salmon to the bowl and let marinate for 20 to 30 minutes.
3. Combine the seasoning ingredients in a small bowl.
4. Place the asparagus and baby corn in separate bowls.
5. Combine the sauce ingredients in a small bowl.
6. Assemble your cooking tray.

Cooking

1. Heat a nonstick wok over high heat for 2 minutes.
2. Carefully spray the wok with the canola oil spray. (If you have a gas stove, turn off the burner before you spray the wok.) Add the salmon with the marinade and stir-fry for 1 minute. Remove from the wok and set aside.
3. Rinse out the wok, then reheat it for 30 seconds. Respray the wok with canola oil spray. Add the seasonings and stir-fry for 15 seconds.
4. Add the asparagus and baby corn and stir-fry for 30 seconds.
5. Stir in the sauce, cover, and cook for 2 minutes.
6. Remove the cover and return the salmon to the wok. Stir to heat through, about 30 seconds.
7. Transfer to a serving platter and garnish with the lemon zest.

■

Each serving provides:
207 Calories
6 g Fat
1 g Saturated Fat
32 mg Cholesterol
18 g Carbohydrate
22 g Protein
267 mg Sodium

■

BAKED TUNA WITH CITRUS-GINGER SAUCE

Makes 4 servings

This zesty citrus sauce adds sparkle and very few calories to the baked fish. You can use salmon or even swordfish, but tuna has the least fat.

Marinade

1/2 cup fresh orange juice
1 tablespoon fresh lime juice
1 tablespoon low-sodium soy sauce
2 teaspoons dry sherry
1 teaspoon minced fresh garlic
1 tablespoon minced fresh ginger
1 tablespoon lime zest
1 tablespoon orange zest

Fish

4 tuna steaks (about 5 ounces each), 1 inch thick

Garnish

Orange slices
Lime slices
Fresh coriander sprigs

Preparation

1. Combine the marinade ingredients in a bowl.
2. Place the tuna in a 9 × 13-inch glass baking dish. Pour the marinade over the fish and let marinate for 30 minutes, turning over the steaks after 15 minutes.

Each serving provides:
226 Calories
3 g Fat
1 g Saturated Fat
81 mg Cholesterol
6 g Carbohydrate
33 g Protein
154 mg Sodium

Cooking

1. Preheat the oven to 450°.
2. Remove the tuna from the marinade and reserve the marinade. Place the steaks on a rack in a baking dish.
3. Bake for 10 minutes, brushing with the reserved marinade after 5 minutes and turning the fish to the other side. (Cook 2 minutes longer for well-done fish.)
4. Transfer the steaks to a serving platter. Spoon the remaining marinade over the steaks and garnish with the orange and lime slices and coriander sprigs.

■ FIVE-SPICE TUNA STEAK

Makes 4 servings

You might wonder why it is necessary to have nine different ingredients in this marinade. The world won't come to an end if you are missing one of these ingredients, but each one, in the Chinese way of things, adds its subtle influence to the flavor, and who is to say which one is not important?

Marinade
2 tablespoons low-sodium soy sauce
2 tablespoons dry sherry
1 tablespoon chili paste
1 teaspoon sesame oil
1 teaspoon sugar
1 teaspoon minced fresh garlic
1 teaspoon minced fresh ginger
1 teaspoon five-spice powder
1/2 teaspoon curry powder

Fish
4 tuna, swordfish, or halibut steaks (about 5 ounces each), 1 inch thick

Additional Ingredients
1/4 cup low-sodium vegetable broth or water
1/2 teaspoon cornstarch dissolved in 1 teaspoon cold water
1 scallion, both white and green parts, chopped

■

Each serving provides:
242 Calories
8 g Fat
2 g Saturated Fat
54 mg Cholesterol
6 g Carbohydrate
33 g Protein
456 mg Sodium

■

Preparation

1. Combine the marinade ingredients and mix well.
2. Place the fish in a 9 × 13-inch glass baking dish. Pour the marinade over the fish. Cover and let marinate overnight, turning the fish occasionally.

Cooking

1. Preheat the oven to 450°.
2. Remove the fish from the marinade and reserve the marinade. Place the tuna in a rack on a baking dish.
3. Bake for 10 to 12 minutes.
4. Meanwhile, combine the reserved marinade with the broth in a small saucepan and bring to a boil.
5. Stir in the cornstarch mixture to thicken. Add the scallions, reduce the heat to low, and cook for 5 minutes.
6. Place the tuna steaks on individual plates and top with the sauce.

■ Spinach-Stuffed Flounder

Makes 4 servings

Steamed fish can be bland, but black bean sauce, a favorite Chinese seasoning, gives this recipe spirit.

1/2 cup chopped onion
1 teaspoon minced fresh garlic
1/2 cup finely chopped red bell pepper
1/2 cup drained canned straw mushrooms
2 teaspoons minced fresh ginger
1 cup low-sodium vegetable or chicken broth
2 teaspoons black bean sauce
1 teaspoon lemon juice
3 cups fresh spinach, well washed and tough stems removed
4 flounder fillets (about 1 pound)
1/4 teaspoon white pepper
1 tablespoon cornstarch dissolved in 2 tablespoons cold water
  Canola oil spray

On Your Tray

- Canola oil spray
- Bowl of onion and garlic
- Bowl of spinach
- Flounder fillets
- White pepper
- Bowl of red pepper, mushrooms, and ginger
- Bowl of broth mixture
- Cornstarch mixture

Preparation

1. Combine the onion and garlic in a small bowl.
2. Combine the red pepper, mushrooms, and ginger in a bowl.
3. Combine the broth, black bean sauce, and lemon juice in another bowl.
4. Assemble your cooking tray.

Cooking

1. Heat a nonstick wok over high heat for 2 minutes.
2. Carefully spray the wok with the canola oil spray. (If you have a gas stove, turn off the burner before you spray the wok.) Add the onion and garlic and stir-fry for 30 seconds.
3. Add the spinach and stir-fry until it wilts, about 1 minute. Remove the spinach from the wok and set it aside in a colander to cool. Rinse out the wok.
4. Place the flounder on a platter, gray side up. Lightly sprinkle the flounder with the white pepper.
5. Place about a 1/4 cup of the drained spinach on each fillet and roll it up, securing it with a bamboo skewer or toothpick.
6. Bring 3 to 4 inches of water to a boil in the wok. Set one rack of a bamboo steamer in the wok.
7. Spray a heatproof plate with canola oil and place the rolled fillets on the plate. Set the plate on the bamboo rack and cover. Steam for 8 minutes.
8. Meanwhile, spray canola oil spray in a small saucepan and sauté the red pepper, straw mushrooms, and ginger for 30 seconds over high heat.
9. Add the broth mixture and bring to a boil.
10. Add the cornstarch mixture and stir for about 30 seconds, until sauce is thickened. Remove the pan from the heat.
11. When the fish is cooked, transfer it to a serving platter and top with the sauce.

■

Each serving provides:
139 Calories
2 g Fat
0.4 g Saturated Fat
60 mg Cholesterol
7 g Carbohydrate
23 g Protein
223 mg Sodium

■

■ GRILLED FISH KABOBS WITH ANISE

Makes 4 servings

Marinade
1/4 cup orange juice
2 tablespoons fresh lemon juice
2 tablespoons low-sodium soy sauce
3 cloves garlic, peeled and coarsely chopped
3 thin slices fresh ginger, each about the size of a quarter

Fish
1 pound swordfish or tuna, cut into 1 1/2-inch cubes

Vegetables
1 anise bulb, stalks removed and cut into 8 wedges
8 large fresh mushrooms, 2 to 3 inches in diameter, cleaned and stems removed
1 medium red onion, peeled and cut into 8 wedges

Additional Ingredients
Canola oil spray
1 seedless orange, thinly sliced for garnish

Preparation

1. Combine the marinade ingredients in a bowl.
2. Add the fish to the bowl and let marinate for 20 to 30 minutes.
3. Bring water to a boil in a saucepan and cook the anise for 3 minutes. Drain and set aside.

■

Each serving provides:
224 Calories
6 g Fat
2 g Saturated Fat
57 mg Cholesterol
12 g Carbohydrate
33 g Protein
330 mg Sodium

■

Assembly

1. Thread the cubes of marinated fish onto 4 bamboo skewers. Reserve the marinade.
2. Thread the vegetables onto 4 separate skewers, alternating the anise wedges, mushroom caps, and onion wedges.

Cooking

1. Lightly spray a preheated grill with canola oil spray.
2. Arrange the skewers on the grill about 4 inches from the heat. Grill the fish 3 to 4 minutes each side, brushing with the reserved marinade. Grill the vegetable skewers a few minutes longer.
3. Remove the fish and vegetables from the skewers and arrange on a serving platter. Strain the reserved marinade. Pour the marinade over the kabobs and arrange the orange slices decoratively around the food.

MAHIMAHI WITH MANGO AND PINEAPPLE

Makes 4 servings

Mahimahi is a good steaming fish because of its delicate flavor and firm flesh. Even though mahimahi and mangoes are not exactly classic Chinese ingredients, they work well in this colorful contemporary recipe.

ON YOUR TRAY

- Bowl of cabbage mixture
- Marinated mahimahi
- Bowl of pineapple
- Bowl of mango
- Bowl of snow peas
- Bowl of just-cooked rice
- Mint sprigs

Marinade

1/4 cup orange juice

1 tablespoon minced fresh ginger

1 tablespoon minced fresh garlic

1 tablespoon low-sodium soy sauce

1 tablespoon dry sherry

Fish

4 pieces mahimahi (about 5 ounces each), 3/4 inch thick, skin and bones removed

Rice

4 cups hot Chinese-Style Boiled Rice (see index)

Cabbage Mixture

2 cups shredded Chinese cabbage

4 scallions, both white and green parts, chopped

1 small onion, chopped

2 tablespoons chopped fresh mint

2 teaspoons minced fresh green chili pepper

1 tablespoon low-sodium soy sauce

Additional Ingredients

2 cups fresh ripe pineapple chunks

2 mangoes, peeled, pitted and cut into 1-inch chunks

2 cups fresh snow peas (about 6 ounces), strings and stems removed

4 fresh mint sprigs for garnish

Preparation

1. Combine the marinade ingredients in a small bowl.
2. Pour the marinade over the fish and let marinate at least 30 minutes, turning it over after 15 minutes.
3. Begin cooking the rice while the fish is marinating. The rice takes about 40 minutes to prepare and will remain hot if the pot is kept covered.
4. Combine the cabbage mixture ingredients in a bowl.
5. Assemble your cooking tray.

Cooking

1. Bring 3 to 4 inches of water to a boil in a wok.
2. Arrange the Chinese cabbage mixture in a heat-proof bowl that fits into a bamboo steamer rack. Place the fish fillets in the bowl and the pineapple and mango over the fish. Cover the steamer. (You may need to divide the ingredients between two steamer racks.)
3. Place the steamer over boiling water in the wok and steam for 10 minutes.
4. Carefully remove the steamer cover and add the snow peas. (Wear oven mitts to avoid being burned by the steam.) Cover and continue to steam 3 more minutes. Remove the wok and steamer from the burner.
5. When cool enough to handle (about 2 minutes), remove the bowl from the steamer. (Wear oven mitts.)
6. Spoon hot rice onto individual plates and top with equal portions of the vegetables, fish, and fruit. Spoon the remaining juices over the top and garnish each serving with a mint sprig.

Each serving provides:
296 Calories
2 g Fat
0.3 g Saturated Fat
71 mg Cholesterol
41 g Carbohydrate
31 g Protein
333 mg Sodium

■ BAKED COD WITH CHINESE CABBAGE

Makes 3 to 4 servings

Cod bakes up nicely in this recipe, but you can substitute another fish if you prefer.

ON YOUR TRAY

- Marinated cod
- Canola oil spray
- Bowl of Chinese cabbage
- Bowl of sauce
- Coriander

Marinade

- 2 tablespoons oyster sauce
- 1 tablespoon dry sherry
- 1 teaspoon minced fresh ginger
- 1 teaspoon minced fresh garlic

Fish

- 1 pound cod fillet, bones removed

Sauce

- 1/4 cup low-sodium vegetable or chicken broth
- 2 tablespoons low-sodium soy sauce
- 2 tablespoons rice vinegar
- 1 teaspoon chili paste

Additional Ingredients

- 1 head Chinese cabbage, washed and thinly sliced into 1/4-inch-wide shreds (about 3 to 4 cups)
- 2 tablespoons chopped fresh coriander leaves for garnish
  Canola oil spray

Preparation

1. Combine the marinade ingredients in a small bowl.
2. Coat both sides of the fillet with the marinade and let marinate for about 30 minutes.
3. Combine the sauce ingredients.
4. Assemble your cooking tray.

■

Each serving provides:
129 Calories
1 g Fat
0.1 g Saturated Fat
48 mg Cholesterol
10 g Carbohydrate
22 g Protein
392 mg Sodium

■

Cooking

1. Preheat the oven to 400°.
2. Wrap the fish in a square of aluminum foil and fold so that none of the juices escape.
3. Place the wrapped fish on a baking sheet and bake for 12 minutes.
4. While the fish is baking, heat a nonstick wok over high heat for 2 minutes.
5. Carefully spray the wok with the canola oil spray. (If you have a gas stove, turn off the burner before you spray the wok.) Add the cabbage and stir-fry for 1 minute.
6. Stir in the sauce and cover. Reduce heat to medium and cook for 3 to 4 minutes, until the cabbage is cooked but still crunchy.
7. Transfer the cabbage to a serving platter. Unwrap the cod fillet, being careful not to lose any of the juices. Place the cod on top of the cabbage. Spoon the cooking juices over the top and sprinkle with the coriander.

NINE

Poultry

Chicken with Three Colorful Peppers

Lemon Chicken

Mu Shu Chicken

Mu Shu Pancakes

Szechuan Chicken with Green Beans and Carrots

Lacquered Chicken Drumsticks

Spicy Chicken and Broccoli

Stir-Fried Chicken and Asparagus

Hoisin Chicken

Roast Chicken with Apricot-Rice Stuffing

Baked Chicken with Almonds

Steamed Chicken and Clams in Black Bean Sauce

Shanghai-Style Braised Turkey Breast

Pineapple Turkey with Snow Peas

Stir-Fried Turkey, Red Peppers, and Shiitake Mushrooms

Poached Turkey Coins with Hoisin

Foolproof Poached Chicken

Turkey with Peaches and Broccoli

Minced Turkey in Lettuce Cups

Steamed Turkey Loaf

■ CHICKEN WITH THREE COLORFUL PEPPERS

Makes 3 to 4 servings

This is a mildly spicy Szechuan recipe—a little chili paste is used, but the peppers are sweet, not hot.

1 tablespoon low-sodium soy sauce
1 tablespoon dry sherry
1 large skinless and boneless chicken breast (about 8 ounces), cut into 3/4-inch pieces

Seasonings
1 tablespoon minced fresh garlic
2 tablespoons minced fresh ginger

ON YOUR TRAY

- Canola oil spray
- Bowl of marinated chicken
- Bowl of seasonings
- Bowl of peppers
- Bowl of sauce
- Cornstarch mixture
- Bowl of peanuts

Peppers and Nuts
1 medium red bell pepper, seeds and ribs removed, cut into 1-inch pieces
1 medium yellow bell pepper, seeds and ribs removed, cut into 1-inch pieces
1 medium green bell pepper, seeds and ribs removed, cut into 1-inch pieces
1/4 cup unsalted dry-roasted peanuts

Sauce
1/2 cup low-sodium chicken broth
1/4 cup dry white wine
1 tablespoon chili paste
1 tablespoon low-sodium soy sauce

Additional Ingredients
1 tablespoon cornstarch dissolved in 2 tablespoons cold water
Canola oil spray

174

Preparation

1. Combine the soy sauce and sherry in a bowl.
2. Add the chicken to the bowl and let marinate for 20 to 30 minutes.
3. Combine the seasoning ingredients in a small bowl.
4. Combine the red, yellow, and green peppers in a bowl. Place the peanuts in a separate bowl.
5. Combine the sauce ingredients in a bowl.
6. Assemble your cooking tray.

Cooking

1. Heat a nonstick wok over high heat for 2 minutes.
2. Carefully spray the wok with the canola oil spray. (If you have a gas stove, turn off the burner before you spray the wok.) Add the chicken and stir-fry for 1 minute. Remove the chicken from the wok and set aside.
3. Rinse out the wok, then reheat it for 30 seconds. Respray the wok with canola oil spray. Add the seasonings and stir-fry for 30 seconds.
4. Add the peppers and stir-fry for 2 minutes.
5. Add the sauce and stir until it comes to a boil.
6. Thicken sauce with the cornstarch mixture if necessary.
7. Return the chicken to the wok and stir about 30 seconds to heat through.
8. Add the peanuts and stir to combine with the chicken and peppers.
9. Remove from the wok and serve.

> ■
>
> Each serving provides:
> 236 Calories
> 7 g Fat
> 2 g Saturated Fat
> 47 mg Cholesterol
> 11 g Carbohydrate
> 21 g Protein
> 408 mg Sodium
>
> ■

■ LEMON CHICKEN

Makes 3 to 4 servings

1 tablespoon dry sherry
1 tablespoon low-sodium soy sauce
2 skinless and boneless chicken breasts (about 12 ounces), cut into 3/4-inch pieces

Seasonings
1 teaspoon minced fresh ginger
1 tablespoon minced fresh garlic

ON YOUR TRAY

- Canola oil spray
- Bowl of marinated chicken
- Bowl of seasonings
- Bowl of carrots
- Bowl of green pepper
- Bowl of scallions
- Bowl of sauce
- Cornstarch mixture

Vegetables
1 large carrot, cut into thin slivers 1 1/2 inches long
1 small green bell pepper, seeds and ribs removed, cut into thin slivers 1 1/2 inches long
8 scallions, both white and green parts, cut into thin slivers 1 1/2 inches long

Sauce
1 cup low-sodium chicken broth
1/4 cup frozen lemonade concentrate
1 tablespoon low-sodium soy sauce
Zest of 1 lemon

Additional Ingredients
1 1/2 tablespoons cornstarch dissolved in 2 tablespoons cold water
Canola oil spray
3 cups thinly shredded crisp lettuce

Preparation

1. Combine the sherry and soy sauce in a bowl.
2. Add the chicken to the bowl and let marinate for 20 to 30 minutes.
3. Combine the seasoning ingredients in a small bowl.
4. Place the carrot, green pepper, and scallions in separate bowls.
5. Combine the sauce ingredients in a bowl.
6. Assemble your cooking tray.

Cooking

1. Heat a nonstick wok over high heat for 2 minutes.
2. Carefully spray the wok with the canola oil spray. (If you have a gas stove, turn off the burner before you spray the wok.) Add the chicken and stir-fry for 1 minute. Remove from the wok and set aside.
3. Rinse out the wok, then reheat it for 30 seconds. Respray the wok with canola oil spray. Add the seasonings and stir-fry for 15 seconds.
4. Add the carrots and stir-fry for 1 minute.
5. Add the green pepper and stir-fry for 1 minute.
6. Add the scallions and stir.
7. Stir in the sauce, cover, and reduce the heat to medium. Cook for 2 minutes.
8. Remove the cover, return the heat to high, and return the chicken to the wok.
9. Add the cornstarch mixture and stir until thickened, about 1 minute.
10. Arrange the lettuce on a serving platter. Pour the chicken mixture over the top and serve.

Each serving provides:
211 Calories
3 g Fat
1 g Saturated Fat
72 mg Cholesterol
15 g Carbohydrate
29 g Protein
280 mg Sodium

■ Mu Shu Chicken

Makes 3 to 4 servings

Mu shu pork is a popular Chinese restaurant selection. Here we substitute chicken for pork because it is lower in fat, but the results are still delicious.

1 tablespoon low-sodium soy sauce

1 tablespoon dry sherry

1/2 teaspoon sugar

8 ounces skinless and boneless chicken breast, cut into
  1/2 × 2-inch julienne

Seasonings

1 tablespoon minced fresh ginger

1 tablespoon minced fresh garlic

On Your Tray

- Canola oil spray
- Bowl of marinated chicken
- Bowl of seasonings
- Bowl of vegetables
- Bowl of sauce
- Scrambled egg substitute

Vegetables

6 dried Chinese mushrooms, soaked in hot water for
  30 minutes

1 cup shredded green cabbage

1 cup grated carrots

6 scallions, both white and green parts, cut into
  1/8 × 2-inch julienne

Egg

1/2 cup liquid egg substitute, lightly beaten

Sauce

1/2 cup low-sodium chicken broth

2 tablespoons hoisin sauce

Additional Ingredients

8 store-bought or homemade mu shu pancakes
  (recipe follows)

1/4 cup hoisin sauce thinned with 1 tablespoon water

8 Scallion Brushes for garnish (see index)
  Canola oil spray

Preparation

1. Combine the soy sauce, sherry, and sugar in a bowl. Mix well, until the sugar is dissolved.
2. Add the chicken to the soy sauce mixture and let marinate for 20 to 30 minutes.
3. Combine the seasoning ingredients in a small bowl.
4. Drain and rinse the mushrooms. Remove and discard the tough stems. Cut the caps into 1/8-inch strips.
5. Combine the mushrooms strips, cabbage, carrots, and scallions in a bowl.
6. Scramble the egg substitute in a nonstick skillet over medium heat. Set aside in a bowl.
7. Combine the sauce ingredients in a bowl.
8. Assemble your cooking tray.

Cooking the Filling

1. Heat a nonstick wok over high heat for 2 minutes.
2. Carefully spray the wok with the canola oil spray. (If you have a gas stove, turn off the burner before you spray the wok.) Add the chicken and stir-fry for 1 minute. Remove the chicken from the wok and set aside.
3. Rinse out the wok, then reheat it for 30 seconds. Respray the wok with canola oil spray. Add the seasonings and stir-fry for 15 seconds.
4. Add the vegetables and stir-fry for 2 minutes.
5. Stir in the sauce, cover, reduce the heat to medium-low, and cook for 3 minutes.
6. Remove the cover, return the chicken to the wok, and stir to heat through.
7. Add the scrambled egg substitute and stir to heat through, about 30 seconds.
8. Remove from the wok and set aside in a bowl.

(continues)

Assembly

1. Bring 3 to 4 inch of water to a boil in the wok.
2. Lightly spray the rack of a bamboo steamer. Carefully separate the pancakes, then restack them and place on the rack of the bamboo steamer.
3. Cover the bamboo steamer, place in the wok over the boiling water, and steam for 5 minutes to heat through.
4. Using a scallion brush, brush a small amount of the thinned hoisin sauce over the surface of the warm pancake.
5. Spoon about 1/3 cup of the chicken mixture in the center of each pancake, top with a scallion brush, and roll up. Eat with your fingers.

■

Each serving provides:
321 Calories
7 g Fat
1 g Saturated Fat
49 mg Cholesterol
37 g Carbohydrate
26 g Protein
335 mg Sodium

■

■ Mu Shu Pancakes

Makes 16 to 18 pancakes, serving 8 to 10

   2 cups all-purpose flour
   1 cup boiling water
   1/4 cup sesame oil

Preparation

1. Place the flour in a mixing bowl and gradually stir in the boiling water. Cover the bowl and set aside for 10 to 15 minutes, or until the dough is cool enough to handle.
2. Turn the dough out on a lightly floured surface and knead with your hands until the dough is smooth and elastic. Add a little more flour if the dough seems sticky.
3. Cover the dough lightly with a dry towel and let it rest about 30 minutes.
4. Roll the dough out on a lightly floured surface to a 1/4-inch thickness.
5. Cut out pancakes using a 3-inch cookie cutter. Reroll the scraps until all the dough has been used.
6. Lightly brush some of the sesame oil on one side of the 3-inch circles.
7. Stack two circles together, oiled sides touching, and carefully roll them out to about a 6-inch diameter. Keep the finished pancakes covered with a towel until cooking so they don't dry out.

Cooking

1. Heat a nonstick skillet over low heat for 1 minute.
2. Cook the pancakes, one at a time, briefly on each side until they bubble slightly. Do not brown.
3. Remove from the skillet and when they are cool enough to handle, gently peel apart the two pancakes.
4. Stack and wrap them securely in foil until ready to use. They may also be frozen at this step.

> ■
>
> Each serving provides:
> 128 Calories
> 5 g Fat
> 0.8 g Saturated Fat
> 1 mg Cholesterol
> 18 g Carbohydrate
> 2 g Protein
> 1 mg Sodium
>
> ■

■ SZECHUAN CHICKEN WITH GREEN BEANS AND CARROTS

Makes 3 to 4 servings

You can control the spiciness of this dish by adjusting the amount of chili peppers. If you like your food spicy-hot, use four peppers. If you want it less hot, use two or three.

1 tablespoon dry sherry

1 teaspoon low-sodium soy sauce

8 ounces skinless and boneless chicken breast, cut into 3/4-inch pieces

Seasonings

2 to 4 whole dried red chili peppers, each 1 1/2 to 2 inches long

1 tablespoon minced fresh ginger

1 tablespoon minced fresh garlic

Vegetables

3 ounces fresh green beans, trimmed and cut into thin slivers

2 medium carrots, peeled and cut into thin slivers

1 small onion, peeled and cut into thin slivers

Additional Ingredients

1/2 cup low-sodium chicken broth

2 tablespoons hoisin sauce

1 teaspoon cornstarch dissolved in 2 teaspoons cold water

Canola oil spray

On Your Tray

- Canola oil spray
- Bowl of marinated chicken
- Bowl of seasonings
- Bowl of vegetables
- Chicken broth
- Hoisin sauce
- Cornstarch mixture

Preparation

1. Combine the sherry and soy sauce in a bowl.
2. Add the chicken to the bowl and let marinate for 20 to 30 minutes.
3. Combine the seasoning ingredients in a small bowl.
4. Combine the green beans, carrots, and onion in a bowl.
5. Assemble your cooking tray.

Cooking

1. Heat a nonstick wok over high heat for 2 minutes.
2. Carefully spray the wok with the canola oil spray. (If you have a gas stove, turn off the burner before you spray the wok.) Add the chicken and stir-fry for 1 minute. Remove the chicken from the wok and set aside.
3. Rinse out the wok, then reheat it for 30 seconds. Respray the wok with canola oil spray. Add the seasonings and stir-fry for 15 seconds.
4. Add the vegetables and stir-fry for 1 minute.
5. Add the chicken broth and cover. Cook for 2 minutes.
6. Remove the cover and return the chicken to the wok. Stir in the hoisin sauce. If necessary, stir in the cornstarch mixture to thicken the sauce.
7. Before serving, remove and discard the chili peppers.

Each serving provides:
176 Calories
2 g Fat
0.6 g Saturated Fat
48 mg Cholesterol
17 g Carbohydrate
20 g Protein
249 mg Sodium

LACQUERED CHICKEN DRUMSTICKS

Makes 4 servings

If you need any proof that chicken drumsticks—without the skin and not fried—can still be a treat, this is it.

3 tablespoons low-sodium soy sauce
2 tablespoons rice vinegar
2 tablespoons brown sugar
1 teaspoon minced fresh garlic
8 chicken drumsticks, skin removed
1 tablespoon cornstarch dissolved in 2 tablespoons cold water

Preparation

1. Combine the soy sauce, rice vinegar, brown sugar, and garlic in a bowl. Mix well, until the sugar is dissolved.
2. Place the drumsticks and the soy sauce mixture in a 9 × 13-inch glass baking dish. Cover with plastic wrap and let the drumsticks marinate overnight in the refrigerator, turning occasionally.

Cooking

1. Remove the drumsticks from the refrigerator 1 hour before roasting to bring up to room temperature.
2. Preheat the oven to 350°.
3. Cover the baking dish with aluminum foil and roast for 1 hour.

Each serving provides:
177 Calories
5 g Fat
1 g Saturated Fat
87 mg Cholesterol
10 g Carbohydrate
24 g Protein
393 mg Sodium

4. Remove the chicken from the oven, drain the juices into a saucepan, and bring to a boil. Use enough of the cornstarch mixture to thicken the sauce.
5. Meanwhile, preheat the oven to broil. Broil the drumsticks about 3 minutes on each side, or until well browned.
6. Serve the drumsticks on a platter and top with the sauce.

SPICY CHICKEN AND BROCCOLI

Makes 3 to 4 servings

This Szechuan dish is mildly spicy, colorful, and tasty. With only two ounces of skinless chicken breast per serving, it is also especially low in fat and calories.

1 tablespoon low-sodium soy sauce
1 tablespoon rice vinegar
8 ounces skinless and boneless chicken breast, cut into 3/4-inch pieces

Seasonings
1 cup finely chopped onion
1 tablespoon minced fresh ginger
1 tablespoon minced fresh garlic

ON YOUR TRAY

- Canola oil spray
- Bowl of marinated chicken
- Bowl of seasonings
- Bowl of vegetables
- Bowl of sauce
- Cornstarch mixture

Vegetables
1/2 red bell pepper, seeds and ribs removed, cut into 1-inch pieces
1/2 green bell pepper, seeds and ribs removed, cut into 1-inch pieces
2 cups broccoli florets

Sauce
1/2 cup low-sodium chicken broth
1 tablespoon dry sherry
1 tablespoon chili paste

Additional Ingredients
1 teaspoon cornstarch dissolved in 2 teaspoons cold water
Canola oil spray

Preparation

1. Combine the soy sauce and rice vinegar in a small bowl.
2. Add the chicken to the bowl and let marinate for 20 to 30 minutes.
3. Combine the seasoning ingredients in a small bowl.
4. Combine the red and green pepper and broccoli in a bowl.
5. Combine the sauce ingredients in a small bowl.
6. Assemble your cooking tray.

Cooking

1. Heat a nonstick wok over high heat for 2 minutes.
2. Carefully spray the wok with the canola oil spray. (If you have a gas stove, turn off the burner before you spray the wok.) Add the chicken and stir-fry for 1 minute. Transfer the chicken to a bowl and set aside.
3. Rinse out the wok, then reheat it for 30 seconds. Respray the wok with canola oil spray. Add the seasonings and stir-fry for 30 seconds.
4. Add the vegetables and stir-fry for 1 minute.
5. Stir in the sauce, cover, and cook for 3 minutes.
6. Remove the cover, return the chicken to the wok, and stir to heat through, about 30 seconds. If necessary, thicken the sauce with the cornstarch mixture.
7. Remove from the wok and serve.

> ■
>
> Each serving provides:
> 148 Calories
> 2 g Fat
> 0.7 g Saturated Fat
> 48 mg Cholesterol
> 11 g Carbohydrate
> 21 g Protein
> 354 mg Sodium
>
> ■

■ STIR-FRIED CHICKEN AND ASPARAGUS

Makes 3 to 4 servings

2 skinless and boneless chicken breasts (about
   12 ounces), cut into 3/4-inch pieces
1 tablespoon low-sodium soy sauce

Seasonings
2 teaspoons minced fresh garlic
2 scallions, both white and green parts, chopped

ON YOUR TRAY

- Canola oil spray
- Bowl of marinated chicken
- Bowl of seasonings
- Bowl of asparagus
- Bowl of sauce
- Cornstarch mixture

Sauce
1 cup low-sodium chicken broth
1 tablespoon dry sherry
1 tablespoon low-sodium soy sauce

Vegetable
2 cups fresh asparagus, trimmed and cut into 1-inch
   pieces on the diagonal

Additional Ingredients
2 teaspoons of cornstarch dissolved in 1 tablespoon
   cold water
   Canola oil spray

Preparation

1. Combine the chicken with the soy sauce and let marinate for 20 to 30 minutes.
2. Combine the seasoning ingredients in a small bowl.
3. Combine the sauce ingredients in another small bowl.
4. Assemble your cooking tray.

Cooking

1. Heat a nonstick wok over high heat for 2 minutes.
2. Carefully spray the wok with the canola oil spray. (If you have a gas stove, turn off the burner before you spray the wok.) Add the chicken and stir-fry for 1 minute. Remove the chicken from the wok and set aside.
3. Rinse out the wok, then reheat it for 30 seconds. Respray the wok with canola oil spray. Add the seasonings and stir-fry for 15 seconds.
4. Add the asparagus and stir-fry for 30 seconds.
5. Add the sauce, cover, and cook 2 minutes.
6. Remove the cover, return the chicken to the wok, and stir to heat through.
7. Pour in the cornstarch mixture and stir until the sauce is slightly thickened, about 30 seconds.
8. Remove from the wok and serve.

Each serving provides:
145 Calories
3 g Fat
1 g Saturated Fat
73 mg Cholesterol
9 g Carbohydrate
17 g Protein
259 mg Sodium

◼ HOISIN CHICKEN

Makes 3 to 4 servings

Hoisin sauce, which is made from soy beans, is a popular Chinese flavoring. It is sweet and a little spicy and gives a distinctive taste to this dish.

2 tablespoons low-sodium soy sauce
1 tablespoon dry sherry
6 ounces skinless and boneless chicken breast, cut into
   3/4-inch pieces

ON YOUR TRAY

- Canola oil spray
- Bowl of marinated chicken
- Bowl of seasonings
- Bowl of blanched broccoli florets
- Hoisin sauce

Seasonings
3 scallions, both white and green parts, finely chopped
1 tablespoon minced fresh ginger
1 tablespoon minced fresh green chili pepper

Additional Ingredients
3 cups broccoli florets
3 tablespoons hoisin sauce
   Canola oil spray

Preparation

1. Combine the soy sauce and sherry in a bowl.
2. Add the chicken to the bowl and let marinate for 20 to 30 minutes.
3. Combine the seasoning ingredients in a small bowl.
4. Bring a saucepan of water to boil. Add the broccoli and cook for 2 minutes. Drain and rinse in cold water. Set aside in a bowl.
5. Assemble your cooking tray.

Cooking

1. Heat a nonstick wok over high heat for 2 minutes.
2. Carefully spray the wok with the canola oil spray. (If you have a gas stove, turn off the burner before you spray the wok.) Add the chicken and stir-fry

◼
Each serving provides:
155 Calories
2 g Fat
0.6 g Saturated Fat
48 mg Cholesterol
12 g Carbohydrate
22 g Protein
321 mg Sodium
◼

for 1 minute. Remove the chicken from the wok and set aside in a bowl.

3. Rinse out the wok, then reheat it for 30 seconds. Respray the wok with canola oil spray. Add the seasonings and stir-fry for 15 seconds.

4. Add the broccoli and stir-fry for 1 minute to heat through.

5. Return the chicken to the wok and stir-fry for 30 seconds to heat through.

6. Stir in the hoisin sauce.

7. Remove from the wok and serve.

ROAST CHICKEN WITH APRICOT-RICE STUFFING

Makes 4 to 6 servings

1 roasting chicken (3½ to 4 pounds)

Stuffing

6 dried Chinese mushrooms, soaked in hot water for
  30 minutes
8 small dried apricots, soaked in ½ cup dry white wine
  or sherry for 10 minutes
½ cup Chinese-Style Boiled Rice (see index)
1 small onion, chopped
½ medium green bell pepper, seeds and ribs removed,
  chopped
1 stalk celery, chopped
3 scallions, both white and green parts, chopped
1 tablespoon minced fresh garlic
1 tablespoon minced fresh ginger

Sauce

¼ cup low-sodium soy sauce
½ teaspoon five-spice powder
  Reserved liquid from the apricots

Additional Ingredient

1 teaspoon sesame oil

■

Each serving provides:
304 Calories
7 g Fat
2 g Saturated Fat
117 mg Cholesterol
14 g Carbohydrate
37 g Protein
488 mg Sodium

■

Preparation

1. Remove the giblets from the chicken. Rinse chicken and pat dry.
2. Drain and rinse the mushrooms. Remove and discard the stems. Coarsely chop the caps.
3. Drain the apricots and reserve the soaking liquid. Coarsely chop the apricots.

4. Combine all the stuffing ingredients in a bowl.
5. Combine the sauce ingredients in a small cup. Add to the stuffing mixture and mix well.

Cooking

1. Preheat the oven to 375°.
2. Fill the cavity of the chicken with the stuffing and tie the legs of the chicken together to prevent the stuffing from falling out.
3. Place the chicken on a rack in a roasting pan and brush the surface of the chicken with the sesame oil.
4. Turn the chicken breast-side down on the rack and roast for 1 hour. Turn the chicken breast-side up and continue roasting another 30 to 45 minutes, or until the skin is golden brown.
5. Before serving, transfer the chicken to a platter and spoon the stuffing into a bowl.

■ Baked Chicken with Almonds

Makes 4 servings

This quick and easy entrée can be served with side dishes of rice and vegetables or on a bed of greens as a warm chicken salad.

16 ounces skinless and boneless chicken breast, trimmed of fat
1 tablespoon low-sodium soy sauce
1 tablespoon dry sherry
2 teaspoons hoisin sauce
2 teaspoons minced fresh ginger
2 teaspoons minced fresh garlic
1 tablespoon sliced almonds (about 1 ounce)

Preparation

1. Rub the soy sauce and sherry on each side of the chicken breasts.
2. Arrange them on a platter and spread the hoisin sauce over each breast. Sprinkle with the ginger and garlic. Prick the surface of each breast with a fork so the flavors will permeate. Set aside for 30 minutes.

Cooking

1. Preheat oven to 375°.
2. Arrange the chicken breasts on a rack on a baking pan. Sprinkle each breast with some of the sliced almonds.
3. Bake for 12 to 15 minutes, depending upon thickness of breasts.
4. Remove to a cutting board and slice each breast on an angle into 8 thin slices.

Each serving provides:
223 Calories
6 g Fat
1 g Saturated Fat
96 mg Cholesterol
4 g Carbohydrate
37 g Protein
229 mg Sodium

■ Steamed Chicken and Clams in Black Bean Sauce

Makes 4 servings

The black bean sauce gives this interesting one-dish meal its distinctive flavor. The chili peppers give it spice.

Marinade
- 1 tablespoon black bean sauce
- 1 tablespoon dry sherry
- 2 teaspoons lemon juice
- 1 teaspoon minced fresh ginger
- 1 teaspoon minced fresh garlic
- 1 teaspoon minced fresh green chili peppers

Chicken
- 8 ounces skinless and boneless chicken breast, cut into 1 1/2-inch cubes

Rice
- 4 cups Chinese-Style Boiled Rice (see index)

Vegetables
- 3 cups bean sprouts, rinsed
- 1/2 cup grated carrots
- 4 scallions, both white and green parts, chopped
- 2 teaspoons minced fresh green chili peppers
- 2 tablespoons minced fresh basil
- 1 teaspoon black bean sauce

Seafood
- 12 small fresh cherrystone clams, scrubbed well

■

Each serving provides:
168 Calories
2 g Fat
0.6 g Saturated Fat
57 mg Cholesterol
12 g Carbohydrate
24 g Protein
249 mg Sodium

■

Preparation

1. Combine all the marinade ingredients in a bowl.
2. Add the chicken to the bowl and let marinate in the refrigerator for 3 hours, or overnight.
3. Begin cooking the rice. It should take about 40 minutes to prepare and will remain hot if the pot is kept covered.
4. Combine all the vegetables in a bowl.

Cooking

1. Bring 3 to 4 inches of water to a boil in a wok.
2. Place the vegetables in a heatproof bowl that will fit in a bamboo steamer rack. Top with the chicken. Tuck the clams, hinge-side up, around the edge of the bowl. (This way, when the clams open, their juices are released on the vegetables and add flavor.) Cover the steamer.
3. Place the steamer over boiling water in the wok and steam for 8 minutes.
4. Carefully remove the steamer from the wok and set aside. When it's cool enough to handle (in about 2 minutes) remove the bowl from the steamer. Wear oven mitts to avoid being burned by the steam.
5. Place equal portions of rice on individual serving plates. Divide the vegetables, chicken, and clams among each plate and spoon the juices over the top.

SHANGHAI-STYLE BRAISED TURKEY BREAST

Turkey is not often found in Chinese recipes or in Chinese restaurants. But in our nutrition-conscious cooking, it is a popular choice. Skinless turkey breast has the lowest fat count of any meat.

Makes 10 to 12 servings

1 fresh turkey breast (6 pounds) with the bone
    (skin removed)

Cooking Liquid
1 cup orange juice
1/4 cup low-sodium soy sauce
1/4 cup dry sherry
2 scallions, both white and green parts, cut into
    3-inch lengths
3 large cloves garlic, peeled and crushed
4 thin slices fresh ginger, each about the size of quarter
2 tablespoons honey
1 tablespoon chili paste
1 tablespoon star anise

Additional Ingredients
Steamed Bread Buns (see index)

1. Rinse the turkey in cold water and pat dry.
2. Combine the cooking liquid ingredients in a bowl.
3. Place the turkey in a covered casserole, which should be just large enough to fit the turkey snugly.
4. Pour in the cooking liquid and add enough water to bring the liquid halfway up the side of the turkey breast. Cover.
5. Place the covered casserole over high heat on top of the stove and bring the liquid to a boil. Reduce the heat to low and simmer for 2 hours. Turn the turkey breast over after 1 hour.

Each turkey serving
provides:
368 Calories
6 g Fat
2 g Saturated Fat
79 mg Cholesterol
36 g Carbohydrate
41 g Protein
315 mg Sodium

6. Remove the turkey from the cooking liquid and allow to cool before carving into thin slices.

7. Strain the cooking liquid into a saucepan. Bring the liquid to a boil and cook until reduced to 1½ to 2 cups.

8. Arrange the sliced turkey on a platter. Serve with the steamed bread buns in a basket and the reduced sauce in a gravy boat. Guests can make sandwiches and spoon a little sauce over the top.

■ PINEAPPLE TURKEY WITH SNOW PEAS

You can use canned pineapple chunks in this recipe, but fresh pineapple is definitely preferred. If using fresh, save the remaining pineapple for a dessert or salad.

1 teaspoon low-sodium soy sauce

1 teaspoon dry sherry

8 ounces skinless and boneless fresh turkey breast, cut into 3/4-inch cubes

Seasonings

1 tablespoon minced fresh ginger

1 tablespoon minced fresh garlic

2 tablespoons minced scallions, both white and green parts

ON YOUR TRAY

- Canola oil spray
- Bowl of marinated turkey
- Bowl of seasonings
- Bowl of snow peas
- Bowl of pineapple
- Bowl of sauce
- Cornstarch mixture

Vegetables and Fruit

1 cup fresh snow peas (about 3 ounces), stems and strings removed

1/2 fresh pineapple, peeled, cored and cut into 1-inch chunks (2 cups)

Sauce

1/4 cup low-sodium chicken broth

3 tablespoons frozen pineapple juice concentrate

1 tablespoon low-sodium soy sauce

1 tablespoon bottled plum sauce

Additional Ingredients

1 teaspoon cornstarch dissolved in 2 teaspoons cold water

Canola oil spray

Preparation

1. Combine the soy sauce and the sherry in a bowl.
2. Add the turkey to the bowl and let marinate for 20 minutes.
3. Combine the seasonings in a small bowl.
4. Place the snow peas and pineapple in separate bowls.
5. Combine the sauce ingredients in a small bowl.
6. Assemble your cooking tray.

Cooking

1. Heat a nonstick wok over high heat for 2 minutes.
2. Carefully spray the wok with the canola oil spray. (If you have a gas stove, turn off the burner before you spray the wok.) Add the turkey and stir-fry for 1 minute. Remove the turkey from the wok and set aside in a bowl.
3. Rinse out the wok, then reheat it for 30 seconds. Respray the wok with canola oil spray. Add the seasonings and stir-fry for 15 seconds.
4. Add the snow peas and stir-fry for 1 minute.
5. Add the pineapple and stir-fry for 10 seconds.
6. Return the turkey to the wok and add the sauce. Stir until heated through, about 1 minute.
7. Thicken the sauce with the cornstarch mixture, if necessary. Remove from the wok and serve.

Each serving provides:
261 Calories
3 g Fat
0.7 g Saturated Fat
48 mg Cholesterol
40 g Carbohydrate
20 g Protein
178 mg Sodium

STIR-FRIED TURKEY, RED PEPPERS, AND SHIITAKE MUSHROOMS

Makes 3 to 4 servings

1 tablespoon low-sodium soy sauce
1 tablespoon dry sherry
8 ounces skinless and boneless fresh turkey breast, cut into 3/4-inch cubes

Seasonings
1 tablespoon minced fresh ginger
1 tablespoon minced fresh garlic

ON YOUR TRAY

- Canola oil spray
- Bowl of marinated turkey
- Bowl of seasonings
- Bowl of mushrooms
- Bowl of red pepper
- Bowl of sauce
- Cornstarch mixture
- Parsley

Vegetables
6 ounces fresh shiitake mushroom caps, cut into 1-inch pieces
1 large red bell pepper, seeds and ribs removed, cut into 1-inch squares

Sauce
1 cup low-sodium chicken broth
2 tablespoons oyster sauce

Additional Ingredients
1 tablespoon cornstarch dissolved in 2 tablespoons cold water
1 tablespoon chopped fresh parsley for garnish
Canola oil spray

Preparation

1. Combine the soy sauce and sherry in a bowl.
2. Add the turkey to the bowl and let marinate for 20 to 30 minutes.
3. Combine the seasoning ingredients in a small bowl.
4. Place the mushrooms and red pepper in separate bowls.
5. Combine the sauce ingredients in a small bowl.
6. Assemble your cooking tray.

Cooking

1. Heat a nonstick wok over high heat for 2 minutes.
2. Carefully spray the wok with the canola oil spray. (If you have a gas stove, turn off the burner before you spray the wok.) Add the turkey and stir-fry for 1 minute. Remove the turkey from the wok and set aside.
3. Rinse out the wok, then reheat it for 30 seconds. Respray the wok with canola oil spray. Add the seasonings and stir-fry for 15 seconds.
4. Add the mushrooms and stir-fry for 1 minute.
5. Add the red pepper and stir-fry for 30 seconds.
6. Stir in the sauce, cover, reduce the heat to medium, and cook for 2 minutes.
7. Remove the cover, add the turkey, and stir to heat through.
8. Add the cornstarch mixture and stir about 30 seconds, or until sauce is thickened.
9. Remove from the wok and sprinkle with the parsley.

Each serving provides:
141 Calories
2 g Fat
0.6 g Saturated Fat
40 mg Cholesterol
10 g Carbohydrate
19 g Protein
186 mg Sodium

■ POACHED TURKEY COINS WITH HOISIN

Makes 4 to 6 servings

Are you ready for this? If you need a special incentive, just imagine the looks of wonder when you bring a steaming platter of Poached Turkey Coins to the dinner table.

2 tablespoons low-sodium soy sauce

1 teaspoon dry sherry

1 pound turkey cutlets, pounded thin (about 6 pieces 3 × 6 × 1/4 inch thick)

1/4 cup finely chopped onion

2 cups tightly packed fresh spinach, washed and tough stems removed

1/2 cup finely chopped fresh mushrooms

1/4 cup finely chopped red bell pepper

1/4 cup Chinese-Style Boiled Rice (see index)

Salt and Pepper to taste

On Your Tray

- Canola oil spray
- Bowl of onion
- Bowl of mushrooms
- Bowl of spinach
- Bowl of red pepper
- Bowl of rice
- Salt and pepper
- Marinated turkey cutlets
- Chicken broth
- Bowl of sauce
- Cornstarch mixture
- Chives

Sauce

1/2 cup strained cooking stock (from poaching turkey)

2 tablespoons hoisin sauce

Additional Ingredients

2 to 3 cups low-sodium chicken broth

2 teaspoons cornstarch dissolved in 1 tablespoon cold water

1 tablespoon chopped chives for garnish

Canola oil spray

Preparation

1. Combine the soy sauce and the sherry in a small bowl.

2. Place the turkey cutlets on a platter. Spoon the soy sauce mixture over the cutlets and let marinate for 20 to 30 minutes.

3. Place the onion, spinach, mushrooms, red pepper, and rice in separate bowls.
4. Combine the sauce ingredients in a small bowl.
5. Assemble your cooking tray.

Cooking

1. Heat a nonstick wok over high heat for 2 minutes.
2. Carefully spray the wok with the canola oil spray. (If you have a gas stove, turn off the burner before you spray the wok.) Add the onions and stir-fry for 30 seconds.
3. Add the mushrooms and stir-fry for 30 seconds.
4. Add the spinach and toss until wilted, about 1 minute.
5. Add the red pepper and stir-fry for 30 seconds.
6. Remove the spinach mixture from the wok to a colander and squeeze to remove excess moisture. Transfer to a mixing bowl mix and add the rice. Toss to combine. Add salt and pepper to taste.
7. Drain the marinade from the turkey and place the cutlets side by side on a large cutting board.
8. Place 2 to 3 tablespoons of the spinach mixture on top of a cutlet leaving about 1 inch of turkey at each end. Starting at one end of the cutlet, carefully roll it into a cylinder and secure with a toothpick or bamboo skewer. Continue filling and rolling all the cutlets.
9. In a skillet just large enough to hold the turkey rolls, bring 2 to 3 cups chicken broth to a boil. Add the turkey rolls. Cover and reduce heat to simmer.
10. Simmer the turkey rolls for 8 to 10 minutes, turning them after 4 to 5 minutes.

(continues)

11. Transfer the rolls to a serving platter and cut each roll into 2 or 3 slices. Reserve the cooking broth and strain it.

12. To make the sauce, combine ½ cup of the reserved cooking broth and the hoisin sauce in a saucepan. Bring to a boil. Stir in the cornstarch mixture to thicken. Pour the sauce over the turkey roll slices.

13. Garnish with the chives and serve.

Each serving provides:
166 Calories
3 g Fat
0.8 g Saturated Fat
64 mg Cholesterol
7 g Carbohydrate
26 g Protein
239 mg Sodium

FOOLPROOF POACHED CHICKEN

Makes 4 to 6 servings

This is an easy, but flavorful, method of cooking chicken. The chicken is perfect in salads, pasta dishes, and sandwiches.

4 chicken breast halves with bones (wings and
     skin removed)
3 slices fresh ginger, peeled and each about the size
     of a quarter
2 large cloves garlic, peeled and slightly smashed
3 scallions, both white and green parts, coarsely chopped

1. Preheat the oven to 350°.
2. Rinse the chicken and pat it dry.
3. Place the chicken, ginger, garlic, and scallions in a heatproof baking dish. Pour in enough cold water to cover the chicken. Cover the dish tightly with foil and bake for 45 minutes (see note).
4. Remove the baking dish from the oven, but do not uncover. Let it cool to room temperature.
5. Uncover the chicken, remove the meat from the bones, and proceed with your recipe, or refrigerate the chicken for later use.

NOTE   If the chicken breasts are not at room temperature when put in the oven, add 10 minutes to the cooking time.

Each serving provides:
200 Calories
4 g Fat
1 g Saturated Fat
96 mg Cholesterol
3 g Carbohydrate
36 g Protein
85 mg Sodium

■ TURKEY WITH PEACHES AND BROCCOLI

Makes 3 to 4 servings

If you think this is an unusual combination for a Chinese recipe, you are right. Life is full of surprises, but not all are as pleasing as this one.

1 tablespoon low-sodium soy sauce

1 tablespoon rice vinegar

8 ounces fresh skinless and boneless turkey breast, cut into 3/4-inch cubes.

Seasonings

1 tablespoon minced fresh green chili pepper

1 tablespoon minced fresh ginger

1 tablespoon minced fresh garlic

1/4 cup finely chopped scallions, both white and green parts

Fruit and Vegetables

2 to 3 firm peaches, peeled, pitted, and cut into 1-inch pieces (1 1/2 cups)

1 1/2 cups broccoli florets

Sauce

1 cup low-sodium chicken broth

1 tablespoon low-sodium soy sauce

Additional Ingredients

1 1/2 tablespoons cornstarch dissolved in 2 tablespoons cold water

Canola oil spray

ON YOUR TRAY

- Canola oil spray
- Bowl of marinated turkey
- Bowl of seasonings
- Bowl of broccoli
- Bowl of sauce
- Bowl of peaches
- Cornstarch mixture

Preparation

1. Combine the soy sauce and rice vinegar in a bowl.
2. Add the turkey to the bowl and let marinate for 20 to 30 minutes.
3. Combine the seasonings in a bowl.
4. Place the peaches and broccoli in separate bowls.
5. Combine the sauce ingredients in a bowl.
6. Assemble your cooking tray.

Cooking

1. Heat a nonstick wok over high heat for 2 minutes.
2. Carefully spray the wok with the canola oil spray. (If you have a gas stove, turn off the burner before you spray the wok.) Add the turkey and stir-fry for 1 minute. Remove from the wok and set aside.
3. Rinse out the wok, then reheat it for 30 seconds. Respray the wok with canola oil spray. Add the seasonings and stir-fry for 15 seconds.
4. Add the broccoli and stir-fry for 30 seconds.
5. Stir in the sauce, cover, reduce the heat to medium, and cook for 3 minutes.
6. Remove the cover, return the heat to high, and add the peaches. Stir-fry for 30 seconds to heat through.
7. Return the turkey to the wok and stir to heat through.
8. Add the cornstarch mixture and stir until thickened, about 30 seconds.
9. Remove from the wok and serve.

■

Each serving provides:
159 Calories
2 g Fat
0.6 g Saturated Fat
40 mg Cholesterol
14 g Carbohydrate
20 g Protein
253 mg Sodium

■

Minced Turkey in Lettuce Cups

Makes 4 servings

This unusual party dish is sure to get the attention of your family or dinner guests.

Marinade
- 1 tablespoon low-sodium soy sauce
- 1 egg white, lightly beaten
- 1 tablespoon oyster sauce
- 1 teaspoon chili paste
- 1 teaspoon cornstarch dissolved in 2 teaspoons cold water

On Your Tray
- Canola oil spray
- Bowl of turkey in marinade
- Bowl of vegetables
- Hoisin sauce
- Lettuce leaves
- Peanuts

Turkey
- 8 ounces ground fresh lean turkey

Vegetables
- 4 dried Chinese mushrooms, soaked in hot water for 30 minutes
- 1/4 cup minced water chestnuts
- 1/4 cup minced onion
- 1 teaspoon minced fresh ginger
- 1 teaspoon minced fresh garlic
- 2 scallions, both white and green parts, finely chopped
- 2 tablespoons minced fresh coriander leaves

Additional Ingredients
- 2 tablespoons hoisin sauce
- 8 to 12 lettuce leaves, washed and dried
- 1/4 cup chopped unsalted peanuts
  Canola oil spray

Preparation

1. Combine the marinade ingredients in a bowl.
2. Add the turkey to the bowl and let marinate for 20 to 30 minutes.
3. Drain and rinse the mushrooms. Remove and discard the stems. Finely chop the mushroom caps.
4. Combine the chopped mushroom and the remaining vegetables in a bowl.
5. Assemble your cooking tray.

Cooking

1. Heat a nonstick wok over high heat for 2 minutes.
2. Carefully spray the wok with the canola oil spray. (If you have a gas stove, turn off the burner before you spray the wok.) Add the turkey and the marinade to the wok and stir-fry for 2 minutes, breaking up any large pieces of meat with a spatula. Remove the turkey to a bowl and set aside.
3. Rinse out the wok, then reheat it for 30 seconds. Respray the wok with canola oil spray. Add the vegetables to the wok and stir-fry for 2 minutes. Be careful not to brown the vegetables, but cook them until the onion is transparent.
4. Return the turkey to the wok and stir to combine it with the vegetables.
5. Add the hoisin sauce and stir-fry for 1 minute. Remove the turkey mixture from the wok.
6. Arrange the lettuce leaves around the edge of a large platter. Mound the turkey mixture in the center. Sprinkle with the peanuts.
7. To serve, each guest places a lettuce leaf on his or her plate, spoons on some of the turkey mixture, and rolls up the lettuce leaf to eat as finger food.

■

Each serving provides:
171 Calories
5 g Fat
0.8 g Saturated Fat
35 mg Cholesterol
13 g Carbohydrate
19 g Protein
278 mg Sodium

■

■ STEAMED TURKEY LOAF

Makes 6 servings

Turkey Mixture

1 pound ground fresh lean turkey

1/2 cup grated carrot

1/2 cup finely chopped green bell pepper

1/2 cup finely chopped onion

1/4 cup chopped scallions, both white and green parts

2 teaspoons minced fresh ginger

2 teaspoons minced fresh garlic

2 egg whites, lightly beaten

2 tablespoons low-sodium soy sauce

Topping

2 tablespoons oyster sauce

2 tablespoons ketchup

Additional Ingredient

2 teaspoons cornstarch dissolved in 2 tablespoons cold water

1. Combine all the turkey mixture ingredients in a bowl.
2. Combine the topping ingredients in a separate bowl.
3. Place the turkey mixture on a heatproof platter that will fit on the rack of a bamboo steamer. Form the turkey into a loaf about 3 inches high by 8 inches long. Spread the topping over the surface. Cover the steamer.
4. Bring 3 to 4 inches of water to a boil in a wok and place the steamer over the boiling water.
5. Steam for 45 to 50 minutes. Check the water level in the wok occasionally. Replenish with boiling water if necessary.

■

Each serving provides:

170 Calories

3 g Fat

0.8 g Saturated Fat

52 mg Cholesterol

9 g Carbohydrate

26 g Protein

280 mg Sodium

■

---

6. Transfer the turkey loaf to a serving platter and keep warm in a low oven.
7. Strain the juices that have collected from the turkey and pour them into a small saucepan. Bring to a boil. Stir in the cornstarch mixture to thicken.
8. Pour the sauce over the turkey loaf and serve.

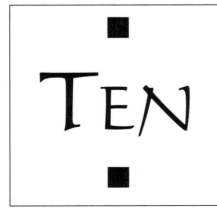

PORK, BEEF, AND LAMB

Peking Pork with Broccoli and Mushrooms

Sweet and Sour Pork

Stir-Fried Hoisin Pork

Pork in Black Bean Sauce

Lemon Pork and Vegetables

Hot and Sour Green Cabbage and Pork

Roast Pork Loin with Ginger-Pineapple Glaze

Coriander-Stuffed Pork Loin

Orange Beef

Stir-Fried Beef and Scallions

Szechuan Beef and Peppers

Beef and Onions in Oyster Sauce

Sliced Steak with Triple Mushroom-Leek Sauce

Peppered Steak with Green Beans and Chives

Beef Steak and Mustard Greens

Fragrant Spiced Beef Roast

Mongolian Lamb and Scallions

Szechuan Lamb with Eggplant and Spinach

Curried Yunnan Lamb

Hunan Lamb

PEKING PORK WITH BROCCOLI AND MUSHROOMS

Makes 3 to 4 servings

Hoisin sauce and five-spice powder contribute their distinctive flavors to this easy stir-fry dish.

8 ounces lean boneless pork loin, cut into 3/4-inch cubes
1 tablespoon low-sodium soy sauce

Seasonings
1 small onion, finely chopped
2 tablespoons minced fresh garlic

ON YOUR TRAY

- Canola oil spray
- Bowl of pork and soy sauce
- Bowl of seasonings
- Bowl of broccoli and mushrooms
- Bowl of sauce
- Hoisin sauce
- Lemon zest

Vegetables
3 cups broccoli florets
8 ounces fresh mushroom caps, about 1 1/2 inches in diameter, cleaned

Sauce
1/2 cup low-sodium chicken broth
1 teaspoon five-spice powder

Additional Ingredients
2 tablespoons hoisin sauce
1 tablespoon lemon zest
Canola oil spray

Preparation

1. Combine the pork and the soy sauce in a bowl and set aside for 20 to 30 minutes.
2. Combine the seasoning ingredients in a small bowl.
3. Combine the broccoli and mushrooms in a bowl.
4. Combine the sauce ingredients in a small bowl.
5. Assemble your cooking tray.

■
Each serving provides:
143 Calories
4 g Fat
2 g Saturated Fat
58 mg Cholesterol
13 g Carbohydrate
15 g Protein
189 mg Sodium
■

Cooking

1. Heat a nonstick wok over high heat for 2 minutes.
2. Carefully spray the wok with the canola oil spray. (If you have a gas stove, turn off the burner before you spray the wok.) Add the pork and stir-fry for 2 minutes, or until the pork loses its pink color. Remove the pork and set aside.
3. Rinse out the wok, then reheat it for 30 seconds. Respray the wok with canola oil spray. Add the seasonings and stir-fry for 30 seconds.
4. Add the broccoli and mushrooms, and stir-fry for 1 minute.
5. Stir in the sauce. Cover and cook for 3 minutes.
6. Remove the cover and return the pork to the wok. Stir-fry to heat through, about 30 seconds.
7. Add the hoisin sauce and lemon zest, and stir to combine with the pork and vegetables.
8. Remove from the wok and serve.

■ SWEET AND SOUR PORK

Makes 3 to 4 servings

In Chinese restaurants, sweet and sour pork is typically deep-fried and thus loaded with fat. In our recipe we stir-fry the pork to reduce the fat, yet the taste is still delicious.

ON YOUR TRAY

- Canola oil spray
- Bowl of pork in marinade
- Bowl of seasonings
- Bowl of peppers and pineapple
- Bowl of sauce

Marinade

- 1 teaspoon low-sodium soy sauce
- 1/2 teaspoon sesame oil
- 1 egg white, lightly beaten
- 1 teaspoon cornstarch

Meat

- 8 ounces lean boneless pork loin, cut into 3/4-inch cubes

Seasonings

- 1 teaspoon minced fresh ginger
- 1 teaspoon minced fresh garlic

Vegetables and Fruit

- 1 medium red bell pepper, seeds and ribs removed, cut into 1-inch squares
- 1 medium green bell pepper, seeds and ribs removed, cut into 1-inch squares
- 2 cups cubed fresh pineapple

Sauce

- 2 tablespoons dry sherry
- 2 tablespoons ketchup
- 2 tablespoons rice vinegar
- 2 tablespoons sugar
- 1 tablespoon low-sodium soy sauce

Additional Ingredients

- Canola oil spray

Preparation

1. Combine the marinade ingredients in a small bowl. Mix well, until the cornstarch is dissolved.
2. Combine the pork with the marinade and set aside for 20 to 30 minutes.
3. Combine the seasoning ingredients in a small bowl.
4. Combine the red and green peppers and the pineapple in a bowl.
5. Combine the sauce ingredients in a small bowl and stir well until the sugar is dissolved.
6. Assemble your cooking tray.

Cooking

1. Heat a nonstick wok over high heat for 2 minutes.
2. Carefully spray the wok with the canola oil spray. (If you have a gas stove, turn off the burner before you spray the wok.) Add the pork and stir-fry for 1 minute. Remove the pork from the wok and set aside.
3. Rinse out the wok, then reheat it for 30 seconds. Respray the wok with canola oil spray. Add the seasonings and stir-fry for 15 seconds.
4. Add the peppers and pineapple and stir-fry for 1 minute.
5. Return the pork to the wok, and stir in the sauce. Cover, lower the heat to medium, and cook for 3 minutes.
6. Remove from the wok and serve.

■

Each serving provides:
229 Calories
6 g Fat
2 g Saturated Fat
48 mg Cholesterol
26 g Carbohydrate
18 g Protein
220 mg Sodium

■

■ STIR-FRIED HOISIN PORK

Makes 4 servings

12 ounces lean boneless pork loin, cut into slices
   1 inch × 2 inches × 1/4 inch thick
2 tablespoons dry sherry

Seasonings
   1 small onion, chopped
   1 tablespoon minced fresh garlic

ON YOUR TRAY

- Canola oil spray
- Bowl with pork in sherry
- Hoisin sauce
- Bowl of seasonings
- Bowl of zucchini and red pepper
- chicken broth

Vegetables
1/2 pound small green zucchini, trimmed and cut into
      1/4-inch rounds
   1 medium red bell pepper, seeds and ribs removed, cut
      into 1-inch squares

Additional Ingredients
1/2 cup low-sodium chicken broth
   2 tablespoons hoisin sauce
      Canola oil spray

Preparation

1. Combine the pork and the sherry in a bowl and let marinate for 20 to 30 minutes.
2. Combine the seasoning ingredients in a small bowl.
3. Combine the zucchini and red pepper in a bowl.
4. Assemble your cooking tray.

Cooking

1. Heat a nonstick wok over high heat for 2 minutes.
2. Carefully spray the wok with the canola oil spray. (If you have a gas stove, turn off the burner before you spray the wok.) Add the pork and stir-fry for 2 minutes, or until it loses its pink color. Remove

the pork from the wok and put it in a bowl. Add the hoisin sauce to the pork and stir to coat. Set aside.

3. Rinse out the wok, then reheat it for 30 seconds. Respray the wok with canola oil spray. Add the seasonings and stir-fry for 30 seconds.
4. Add the zucchini and red pepper and stir-fry for 30 seconds.
5. Add the chicken broth, cover, and simmer for 2 minutes.
6. Remove the cover, return the pork to the wok, and stir about 30 seconds to heat through.
7. Remove from the wok and serve.

Each serving provides:
219 Calories
7 g Fat
2 g Saturated Fat
78 mg Cholesterol
8 g Carbohydrate
24 g Protein
98 mg Sodium

PORK IN BLACK BEAN SAUCE

Makes 3 to 4 servings

This alternative to traditional spare ribs is much lower in fat. We use lean pork instead of ribs and reduce the amount of meat per serving by adding sweet peppers and spinach.

1 tablespoon dry sherry

1 teaspoon low-sodium soy sauce

12 ounces lean boneless pork loin, cut into 3/4-inch cubes

Seasonings

1 tablespoon minced fresh ginger

1 tablespoon minced fresh garlic

1 tablespoon minced fresh green chili pepper

ON YOUR TRAY

- Canola oil spray
- Bowl of marinated pork
- Bowl of seasonings
- Bowl of red and yellow peppers
- Bowl of spinach
- Bowl of sauce
- Cornstarch mixture
- Scallions

Vegetables

1 medium yellow bell pepper, seeds and ribs removed, and cut into 1-inch squares

1 medium red bell pepper, seeds and ribs removed, and cut into 1-inch squares

2 cups tightly packed fresh spinach, washed well and tough stems removed

Sauce

1 cup low-sodium chicken broth

2 tablespoons black bean sauce

Additional Ingredients

1 tablespoon cornstarch dissolved in 2 tablespoons cold water

2 scallions, both white and green parts, thinly sliced for garnish

Canola oil spray

Preparation

1. Combine the sherry and the soy sauce in a bowl.
2. Add the pork to the bowl and let marinate for 20 to 30 minutes.
3. Combine the seasoning ingredients in a small bowl.
4. Place the yellow and red peppers in one bowl and the spinach in a separate bowl.
5. Combine the sauce ingredients in a bowl and mix well.
6. Assemble your cooking tray.

Cooking

1. Heat a nonstick wok over high heat for 2 minutes.
2. Carefully spray the wok with the canola oil spray. (If you have a gas stove, turn off the burner before you spray the wok.) Add the pork and stir-fry for 2 minutes, or until it loses its pink color. Remove the pork from the wok and set aside.
3. Rinse out the wok, then reheat it for 30 seconds. Respray the wok with canola oil spray. Add the seasonings and stir-fry for 15 seconds.
4. Add the red and yellow peppers and stir-fry for 30 seconds.
5. Add the spinach and toss until it wilts.
6. Add the sauce and stir. Cover and cook for 1 minute.
7. Remove the cover, return the pork to the wok, and stir to heat through.
8. Add the cornstarch mixture and stir until the sauce is thickened, about 30 seconds.
9. Transfer to a serving platter and sprinkle with the scallions.

Each serving provides:
238 Calories
7 g Fat
2 g Saturated Fat
76 mg Cholesterol
13 g Carbohydrate
27 g Protein
429 mg Sodium

■ LEMON PORK AND VEGETABLES

Makes 3 to 4 servings

The pork found in markets these days can be very bland, but lemon, garlic, and hoisin sauce bring zest to this recipe.

1 tablespoon fresh lemon juice
1 tablespoon low-sodium soy sauce
1/2 teaspoon sugar
8 ounces lean boneless pork loin, cut into thin shreds 2 inches long

Vegetables
1/2 pound thin asparagus, trimmed and cut into 2-inch lengths
1/2 cup sliced water chestnuts

ON YOUR TRAY

- Canola oil spray
- Bowl of marinated pork
- Garlic
- Bowl of asparagus and water chestnuts
- Bowl of sauce

Sauce
1/2 cup low-sodium chicken broth
2 tablespoons lemon zest
2 tablespoons hoisin sauce
1 tablespoon fresh lemon juice

Additional Ingredients
1 tablespoon minced fresh garlic
Canola oil spray

Preparation

1. Combine the lemon juice, soy sauce, and sugar in a bowl. Mix well until the sugar is dissolved.
2. Add the pork to the bowl and let marinate for 20 to 30 minutes.

3. Combine the asparagus and water chestnuts in a bowl.
4. Combine the sauce ingredients in a bowl.
5. Assemble your cooking tray.

Cooking

1. Heat a nonstick wok over high heat for 2 minutes.
2. Carefully spray the wok with the canola oil spray. (If you have a gas stove, turn off the burner before you spray the wok.) Add the pork and stir-fry for 1 minute. Remove the pork from the wok and set aside in a bowl.
3. Rinse out the wok, then reheat it for 30 seconds. Respray the wok with canola oil spray. Add the garlic and stir-fry for 15 seconds.
4. Add the asparagus and water chestnuts and stir-fry for 1 minute.
5. Add the sauce, stir, and cover. Cook for 2 minutes.
6. Remove the cover, return the pork to the wok, and stir about 30 seconds to heat through.
7. Remove from the wok and serve.

■

Each serving provides:
142 Calories
4 g Fat
2 g Saturated Fat
58 mg Cholesterol
12 g Carbohydrate
14 g Protein
174 mg Sodium

■

■ HOT AND SOUR GREEN CABBAGE AND PORK

Makes 3 to 4 servings

In this recipe, the chili pepper is the "hot" component and the rice vinegar is the "sour" one. You can vary the hot-sour balance, if you wish, by adjusting the amount of these two ingredients.

8 ounces lean boneless pork loin, cut into thin shreds 2 inches long
2 tablespoons low-sodium soy sauce

Seasonings

2 tablespoons minced fresh green chili peppers
1 tablespoon minced fresh ginger
1 tablespoon minced fresh garlic

ON YOUR TRAY

- Canola oil spray
- Bowl of marinated pork
- Bowl of seasonings
- Bowl of vegetables
- Bowl of sauce

Vegetables

3 cups coarsely chopped fresh green cabbage
1 medium carrot, peeled and cut into 1/2-inch cubes
6 scallions, both white and green parts, chopped

Sauce

1/4 cup low-sodium chicken broth or water
3 tablespoons rice vinegar
2 teaspoons sugar
1 teaspoon chili paste

Additional Ingredient

Canola oil spray

■

Each serving provides:
146 Calories
4 g Fat
2 g Saturated Fat
58 mg Cholesterol
13 g Carbohydrate
13 g Protein
308 mg Sodium

■

Preparation

1. Combine the pork and soy sauce in a bowl and set aside for 20 to 30 minutes.
2. Combine the seasoning ingredients in a small bowl.
3. Combine the vegetables in a bowl.

4. Combine the sauce ingredients in a small bowl.
5. Assemble your cooking tray.

Cooking

1. Heat a nonstick wok over high heat for 2 minutes.
2. Carefully spray the wok with the canola oil spray. (If you have a gas stove, turn off the burner before you spray the wok.) Add the pork and stir-fry for 1 minute, or until it loses its pink color. Remove the pork from the wok and set aside in a bowl.
3. Rinse out the wok, then reheat it for 30 seconds. Respray the wok with canola oil spray. Add the seasonings and stir-fry for 15 seconds.
4. Add the vegetables and stir-fry for 30 seconds.
5. Stir in the sauce, cover, and simmer for 3 minutes.
6. Remove the cover and return the pork to the wok. Stir about 30 seconds, or until the pork is heated through.
7. Remove from the wok and serve.

ROAST PORK LOIN WITH GINGER-PINEAPPLE GLAZE

Makes 4 to 6 servings

Marinade

- 1 cup unsweetened pineapple juice
- 2 tablespoons minced fresh ginger
- 1 tablespoon minced fresh garlic
- 1 tablespoon low-sodium soy sauce

Meat

- 1½ pound center cut boneless pork loin, trimmed of fat
- 1 teaspoon sesame oil

Sauce

- 1 tablespoon dark brown sugar
  Reserved marinade
- 4 slices fresh or canned pineapple, cut into
  1-inch pieces

Additional Ingredient

- 1 tablespoon cornstarch dissolved in 2 tablespoons
  cold water

1. Combine the marinade ingredients in a small bowl.
2. Place the pork roast in a glass or stainless steel pan that fits it snugly, such as a meatloaf pan. Pierce the surface of the roast with a fork. Pour the marinade over the roast and cover. Let the roast marinate for at least 3 hours, or overnight in the refrigerator, turning the meat occasionally.
3. Remove the roast from the pan and reserve the marinade. (If the roast has been refrigerated, allow it to return to room temperature for 1 hour before roasting.) Strain the marinade to remove the garlic and ginger and set aside.

■

Each serving provides:
293 Calories
10 g Fat
3 g Saturated Fat
96 mg Cholesterol
17 g Carbohydrate
33 g Protein
135 mg Sodium

■

PORK, BEEF, AND LAMB

4. Preheat the oven to 375°.
5. Place the pork on a rack in a roasting pan and brush with the sesame oil.
6. Roast for 1 hour and 15 minutes, or until a meat thermometer reaches 160°.
7. Combine the sauce ingredients in a small saucepan. Bring the sauce to a boil. Add the cornstarch mixture and stir to thicken.
8. Slice the pork and arrange it on a serving platter. Pour the sauce over the pork slices.

PORK, BEEF, AND LAMB

CORIANDER-STUFFED PORK LOIN

Makes 4 to 6 servings

Coriander gives this pork roast a distinctive herbed flavor.

Stuffing

- 1/2 cup minced coriander leaves
- 1/4 cup pine nuts, lightly browned in a dry skillet ove medium heat
- 2 scallions, both white and green parts, minced
- 3 tablespoons low-sodium soy sauce
- 1 fresh green chili pepper, minced
- 1 tablespoon fresh lemon juice
- 1 tablespoon lemon zest
- 1 tablespoon sugar
- 1 tablespoon minced fresh ginger
- 1 teaspoon minced fresh garlic

Meat

1 1/2 pound center cut boneless pork loin, trimmed of fat

Preparation

1. Combine all the stuffing ingredients in a blender or food processor and blend to make a wet paste.
2. Place the pork loin on a cutting board. Make a cut from end to end down the center of the roast, but do not cut all the way through. The roast will open like a book. Make similar cuts from end to end on either side of the center cut so that the roast lies flat on the cutting board.
3. Spread three-quarters of the stuffing over the surface of the roast. Roll the roast closed and tie with butcher string at 3-inch intervals.

Each serving provides:
310 Calories
13 g Fat
4 g Saturated Fat
112 mg Cholesterol
6 g Carbohydrate
39 g Protein
277 mg Sodium

PORK, BEEF, AND LAMB

4. Place the roast in a pan slightly larger than the meat. Spread the remaining stuffing mixture over the top of the roast. Cover with plastic wrap and refrigerate overnight.

Cooking

1. Remove the roast from the refrigerator 1 hour before roasting to bring to room temperature.
2. Preheat oven to 375°.
3. Place the pork on a rack in a roasting pan.
4. Roast for 1 hour and 15 minutes to 1 1/2 hours, or until a meat thermometer registers 160°.
5. Remove the pork to a cutting board. Allow it to rest for 10 minutes. Remove the strings and cut into 1-inch slices.

■ Orange Beef

Makes 3 to 4 servings

1 tablespoon low-sodium soy sauce
1 tablespoon dry sherry
8 ounces lean flank steak, cut into slices 1 inch ×
   1 inch × 1/8 inch thick (see note)

Seasonings
1/2 onion, finely chopped
2 tablespoons minced orange peel
1 to 2 tablespoons minced fresh green chili pepper
1 tablespoon minced fresh garlic
1 tablespoon minced fresh ginger

ON YOUR TRAY

- Canola oil spray
- Bowl of marinated beef
- Bowl of seasonings
- Bowl of celery
- Bowl of mushrooms
- Bowl of red pepper
- Bowl of sauce
- Cornstarch mixture

Vegetables
8 dried Chinese mushrooms, soaked in hot water for
   30 minutes
2 stalks celery, sliced on the diagonal 1/8 inch thick
2 medium red bell peppers, seeds and ribs removed, and
   cut into thin slices 1/8 inch wide × 2 inches long

Sauce
1/2 cup low-sodium beef broth
2 tablespoons frozen orange juice concentrate
1 tablespoon low-sodium soy sauce

Additional Ingredients
1 teaspoon cornstarch dissolved in 1 tablespoon
   cold water
Canola oil spray

Preparation

1. Combine the soy sauce and sherry in a bowl.
2. Add the steak to the bowl and let marinate for
   20 to 30 minutes.

3. Combine the seasoning ingredients in a bowl.
4. Drain the mushrooms and rinse them. Remove and discard the tough stems. Slice the caps into thin strips 1/8 inch wide.
5. Place the mushroom cap strips, the celery, and red pepper in separate bowls.
6. Combine the sauce ingredients in a bowl.
7. Assemble your cooking tray.

Cooking

1. Heat a nonstick wok over high heat for 2 minutes.
2. Carefully spray the wok with the canola oil spray. (If you have a gas stove, turn off the burner before you spray the wok.) Add the beef and stir-fry for 1 minute. Remove from the wok and set aside.
3. Rinse out the wok, then reheat it for 30 seconds. Respray the wok with canola oil spray. Add the seasonings and stir-fry for 30 seconds.
4. Add the celery and stir-fry for 1 minute.
5. Add the mushrooms and stir-fry for 1 minute.
6. Add the red pepper and stir-fry for 1 minute.
7. Add the sauce and bring to a boil.
8. Return the beef to the wok and stir to heat through.
9. Add the cornstarch mixture and stir until thickened, about 30 seconds.
10. Remove from the wok and serve.

NOTE   For ease in slicing flank steak, follow these instructions: Trim off the fat and cut the steak into 3 long strips about 2 inches wide, following the grain. Wrap each strip individually in foil and place in the freezer for 1 hour. Slice according to recipe instructions.

■

Each serving provides:
149 Calories
4 g Fat
2 g Saturated Fat
50 mg Cholesterol
15 g Carbohydrate
18 g Protein
253 mg Sodium

■

PORK, BEEF, AND LAMB

233

■ Stir-Fried Beef and Scallions

Makes 3 to 4 servings

1 tablespoon low-sodium soy sauce
1 tablespoon dry sherry
1 teaspoon sesame oil
12 ounces flank steak, trimmed of fat and cut into thin slices across the grain, 2 inches × 2 inches × 1/8 inch thick (see note)

Seasonings

1/4 cup finely chopped onion
2 tablespoons minced fresh green chili pepper
1 tablespoon minced fresh ginger
1 tablespoon minced fresh garlic

On Your Tray

- Canola oil spray
- Bowl of marinated beef
- Bowl of seasonings
- Bowl of mushrooms
- Bowl of sauce
- Bowl of scallions
- Cornstarch mixture
- Parsley

Vegetables

12 scallions, both white and green parts, cut into thin strips, 2 inches long
8 ounces large fresh mushrooms, cleaned, trimmed, and cut into 1/4-inch slices

Sauce

1 cup low-sodium beef or chicken broth
1 tablespoon low-sodium soy sauce
2 teaspoons sugar

Additional Ingredients

2 teaspoons cornstarch dissolved in 1 tablespoon cold water
2 tablespoons chopped fresh parsley for garnish
Canola oil spray

Preparation

1. Combine the soy sauce, sherry, and the sesame oil in a bowl.
2. Add the steak to the bowl and let marinate for 20 to 30 minutes.
3. Combine the seasonings in a bowl.
4. Place the scallions and mushrooms in separate bowls.
5. Combine the sauce ingredients in a bowl.
6. Assemble your cooking tray.

Cooking

1. Heat a nonstick wok over high heat for 2 minutes.
2. Carefully spray the wok with the canola oil spray. (If you have a gas stove, turn off the burner before you spray the wok.) Add the beef and stir-fry for 1 minute. Remove the beef to a bowl and set aside.
3. Rinse out the wok, then reheat it for 30 seconds. Respray the wok with canola oil spray. Add the seasonings and stir-fry for 15 seconds.
4. Add the mushrooms and stir-fry for 45 seconds.
5. Add the sauce, cover, and cook for 1 minute.
6. Remove the cover, add the scallions, and stir to combine.
7. Return the beef to the wok and stir to heat through.
8. Add the cornstarch mixture and stir to thicken, about 30 seconds.
9. Remove from the wok and sprinkle with the parsley.

NOTE   For ease in slicing flank steak follow these instructions: Trim off the fat and cut the steak into 3 long strips about 2 inches wide, following the grain. Wrap each strip individually in foil and place in the freezer for 1 hour. Slice according to recipe instructions.

Each serving provides:
249 Calories
8 g Fat
3 g Saturated Fat
75 mg Cholesterol
15 g Carbohydrate
30 g Protein
270 mg Sodium

■ Szechuan Beef and Peppers

Makes 3 to 4 servings

There is a serious amount of chili pepper in this recipe—you'll be sure to notice the fumes when you stir-fry them. If you prefer this dish less hot, use only two chili peppers.

1 tablespoon dry sherry
1 tablespoon low-sodium soy sauce
8 ounces flank steak, trimmed of fat and cut into thin slices across the grain, 2 inches × 2 inches × 1/8 inch thick (see note)

Seasonings
1 cup finely chopped onion
1 tablespoon minced fresh garlic
1 tablespoon minced fresh ginger

On Your Tray

- Canola oil spray
- Bowl of marinated beef
- Bowl of dried chili peppers
- Bowl of seasonings
- Bowl of bell peppers
- Bowl of sauce
- Cornstarch mixture

Peppers
3 to 4 dried red chili peppers, each 1 1/2 to 2 inches long
1 large red bell pepper, seeds and ribs removed, and cut into 1/8 × 2-inch slivers
1 large yellow bell pepper, seeds and ribs removed, and cut into 1/8 × 2-inch slivers
1 large green bell pepper, seeds and ribs removed, and cut into 1/8 × 2-inch slivers

Sauce
1/2 cup low-sodium beef or chicken broth
2 tablespoons dry sherry
1 tablespoon low-sodium soy sauce
1 tablespoon rice vinegar
2 teaspoons sugar
1 teaspoon chili paste

Additional Ingredients
1 teaspoon cornstarch dissolved in 2 teaspoons cold water
Canola oil spray

236

Preparation

1. Combine the sherry and soy sauce in a bowl.
2. Add the beef to the bowl and let marinate for 20 to 30 minutes.
3. Combine the seasoning ingredients in a small bowl.
4. Place the chili peppers in a bowl. Combine the red, yellow, and green bell peppers in another bowl.
5. Combine the sauce ingredients in a bowl.
6. Assemble your cooking tray.

Cooking

1. Heat a nonstick wok over high heat for 2 minutes.
2. Carefully spray the wok with the canola oil spray. (If you have a gas stove, turn off the burner before you spray the wok.) Add the beef and stir-fry for 1 minute. Remove the beef from the wok and set aside.
3. Rinse out the wok, then reheat it for 30 seconds. Respray the wok with canola oil spray. Add the dried chili peppers and stir-fry for 15 seconds.
4. Add the seasonings and stir-fry for 1 minute.
5. Add the bell peppers and stir-fry for 1 minute.
6. Add the sauce and stir to combine, about 15 seconds.
7. Return the beef to the wok and stir to heat through.
8. Add the cornstarch mixture and stir until the sauce is slightly thickened, about 30 seconds.
9. Transfer to a serving platter. Remove and discard the dried chili peppers before serving.

NOTE   For ease in slicing flank steak, follow these instructions: Trim off the fat and cut the steak into 3 long strips about 2 inches wide, following the grain. Wrap each strip individually in foil and place in the freezer for 1 hour. Slice according to recipe instructions.

Each serving provides:
160 Calories
5 g Fat
2 g Saturated Fat
43 mg Cholesterol
14 g Carbohydrate
13 g Protein
299 mg Sodium

■ BEEF AND ONIONS IN OYSTER SAUCE

Makes 3 to 4 servings

1 tablespoon dry sherry

1 teaspoon low-sodium soy sauce

8 ounces lean flank steak, thinly sliced across the grain into pieces 2 inches × 2 inches × 1/8 inch thick (see note)

Seasonings

1 tablespoon minced fresh ginger

1 teaspoon minced fresh garlic

ON YOUR TRAY

- Canola oil spray
- Bowl of marinated beef
- Bowl of seasonings
- Bowl of onions
- Bowl of celery
- Bowl of sauce
- Bowl of tomatoes

Vegetables

4 medium onions, cut into 8 wedges each

2 stalks celery, cut into 1/4-inch slices on the diagonal

2 medium tomatoes, cut into 8 wedges each

Sauce

1/2 cup low-sodium beef stock

3 tablespoons oyster sauce

3 tablespoons ketchup

Additional Ingredient

Canola oil spray

Preparation

1. Combine the sherry and soy sauce in a bowl.
2. Add the beef to the bowl and let marinate for 20 to 30 minutes.
3. Combine the seasonings in a bowl.
4. Place the onions, celery, and tomatoes in separate bowls.
5. Combine the sauce ingredients in a small bowl.
6. Assemble your cooking tray.

Cooking

1. Heat a nonstick wok over high heat for 2 minutes.
2. Carefully coat the bottom with canola oil spray (If you have a gas stove, turn off the burner before you spray the wok.) Add the beef and stir-fry for 1 minute. Remove the beef from the wok and set aside.
3. Rinse out the wok, then reheat it for 30 seconds. Respray the wok with canola oil spray. Add the seasonings and stir-fry for 15 seconds.
4. Add the onions, tossing and separating the pieces while stir-frying for 2 minutes.
5. Add the celery and stir-fry for 2 minutes.
6. Add the sauce, cover and simmer 2 minutes.
7. Remove the cover, add the tomatoes, and cook for 1 minute.
8. Return the beef to the wok and stir about 30 seconds to heat through.
9. Remove from the wok and serve.

NOTE   For ease in slicing flank steak, follow these instructions: Trim off the fat and cut the steak into 3 long strips about 2 inches wide, following the grain. Wrap each strip individually in foil and place in the freezer for 1 hour. Slice according to recipe instructions.

Each serving provides:
197 Calories
5 g Fat
2 g Saturated Fat
50 mg Cholesterol
19 g Carbohydrate
21 g Protein
281 mg Sodium

Sliced Steak with Triple Mushroom-Leek Sauce

Makes 4 to 6 servings

Grilled steak is not a typical Chinese food, and steak may be an unexpected choice for a fat-conscious cookbook, but life is full of surprises and exceptions. For many of us, no matter how careful we are about nutrition, there is still a time for a special steak dinner. In this recipe, the marinade acts as a meat tenderizer and the sauce and mushrooms add a Chinese flavor.

On Your Tray

- Bowl of marinated steak
- Canola oil spray
- Bowl of vegetables
- Bowl of sauce

Marinade

1/2 cup dry white wine or dry sherry
2 tablespoons low-sodium soy sauce
1 tablespoon minced fresh ginger
1 teaspoon minced fresh garlic

Meat

1 1/2 pound boneless sirloin steak, at least 1 1/2 inches thick and trimmed of fat

Vegetables

1/2 cup dried Chinese mushrooms, soaked in hot water for 30 minutes
1 cup fresh shiitake mushrooms
2 leeks
1 cup drained canned straw mushrooms
1/2 cup canned or fresh water chestnuts, peeled and sliced

Sauce

2 tablespoons hoisin sauce
1 tablespoon black bean sauce
1 tablespoon rice vinegar
2 teaspoons chili paste
Reserved marinade

Additional Ingredient

Canola oil spray

Preparation

1. Combine the marinade ingredients and mix well.
2. Place the steak in a shallow bowl and pour the marinade over it. Cover and refrigerate for 3 hours, or overnight. Drain and reserve the marinade.
3. Remove the dried mushrooms from their soaking liquid. Rinse and drain them. Remove and discard the tough stems. Slice the caps.
4. Remove and discard the stems of the shiitake mushrooms. Slice the caps 1/8 inch thick.
5. Trim the root end of each leek. Cut off and discard the upper green part of the leek, about 2 inches above the white bulb. Make a slit in the remaining part of each leek and rinse well under cold running water to remove any sand that has lodged in the leaves. Thinly slice the leeks.
6. Combine all the vegetables in a bowl.
7. Combine the sauce ingredients in a bowl.
8. Assemble your cooking tray.

Cooking

1. Grill or broil the steak medium-rare. Set aside and keep warm in a low oven while you prepare the sauce.
2. Heat a nonstick wok over high heat for 2 minutes.
3. Carefully spray the wok with the canola oil spray. (If you have a gas stove, turn off the burner before you spray the wok.) Add the vegetables and stir-fry for 2 minutes.
4. Add the sauce and bring to a boil. Remove the wok from the heat.
5. Slice the steak thinly across the grain and arrange on a serving platter.
6. Pour the mushroom-leek sauce over the steak and serve.

> ■
>
> Each serving provides:
> 224 Calories
> 9 g Fat
> 4 g Saturated Fat
> 101 mg Cholesterol
> 8 g Carbohydrate
> 34 g Protein
> 398 mg Sodium
>
> ■

Peppered Steak with Green Beans and Chives

Makes 4 servings

On Your Tray

- Canola oil spray
- Marinated steak coated with peppercorns
- Bowl of seasonings
- Bowl of green beans
- Bowl of sauce
- Reserved marinade
- Chives

Marinade

- 2 tablespoons hoisin sauce
- 1 tablespoon dry sherry
- 1 teaspoon minced fresh ginger
- 1 teaspoon minced fresh garlic
- 1 scallion, both white and green part, minced

Meat

- 1 lean strip steak (about 12 ounces), 1/2 inch thick
- 2 tablespoons mixed peppercorns (white, black, pink, and green) or black peppercorns

Seasonings

- 1 teaspoon minced fresh garlic
- 1 teaspoon minced fresh ginger

Sauce

- 1/2 cup low-sodium beef or chicken broth
- 1 tablespoon low-sodium soy sauce
- 1 tablespoon dry sherry

Additional Ingredients

- 8 ounces fresh green beans, trimmed and cut into 2-inch slivers
- 2 tablespoons chopped fresh chives for garnish
  Canola oil spray

Preparation

1. Combine the marinade ingredients in a bowl.
2. Coat the steak with the marinade. Cover and re-frigerate at least 3 hours, or overnight. Turn the steak over occasionally.
3. Stir-fry the peppercorns in a dry hot skillet until they begin to pop, about 2 minutes. Coarsely grind the peppercorns in a pepper mill or with a mortar and pestle.
4. Remove the steak from the marinade and reserve the marinade. Coat both sides of the steak with the crushed peppercorns.
5. Combine the seasoning ingredients in a small bowl.
6. Combine the sauce ingredients in a small bowl.
7. Assemble your cooking tray.

Cooking

1. Heat a nonstick wok over high heat for 2 minutes.
2. Carefully spray the wok with the canola oil spray. (If you have a gas stove, turn off the burner before you spray the wok.) Sear the steak 2 minutes on each side and transfer to a cutting board.
3. Rinse out the wok, then reheat it for 30 seconds. Respray the wok with canola oil spray. Add the seasonings and stir-fry for 15 seconds.
4. Add the green beans and stir-fry for 1 minute.
5. Add the sauce, cover, reduce the heat to medium-low, and cook for 3 minutes.
6. Meanwhile, slice the steak on the diagonal across the grain into slices 1/4 inch thick.
7. Return the meat to the wok, add the reserved marinade, and cook for 1 minute.
8. Remove from the wok. Sprinkle with the chives and serve.

■

Each serving provides:
211 Calories
7 g Fat
3 g Saturated Fat
76 mg Cholesterol
10 g Carbohydrate
28 g Protein
379 mg Sodium

■

■ BEEF STEAK AND MUSTARD GREENS

Makes 4 servings

This recipe (not surprisingly) comes up on the high end of almost all of our nutritional category counts. But if you have been good the rest of the day and you're in the mood for steak, you should be able to fit this into your fat and calorie budgets.

4 boneless steaks (about 8 ounces each; club or shell steaks work well), 1/2 inch thick and trimmed of fat

4 teaspoons low-sodium soy sauce
Black pepper to taste

2 cups tightly packed mustard greens, arugula, or watercress, washed and trimmed

Seasonings

1/2 cup finely chopped onion

2 teaspoons minced fresh ginger

1 teaspoon minced fresh garlic

1 teaspoon minced fresh green chili pepper

ON YOUR TRAY

- Platter of seasoned steaks
- Canola oil spray
- Bowl of seasonings
- Bowl of sauce
- Chives

Sauce

1/2 cup low-sodium beef or chicken broth

2 tablespoons ketchup

2 tablespoons hoisin sauce

Additional Ingredients

1 tablespoon finely chopped fresh chives for garnish
Canola oil spray

Preparation

1. Spoon ½ teaspoon of the soy sauce on each side of the 4 steaks and brush to coat the surface. Sprinkle each side with black pepper. Set aside the steaks for 20 to 30 minutes.
2. Bring 2 quarts of water to a boil to blanch the greens. When water has come to a boil, add the greens, stir them around, and immediately remove and drain. Set aside.
3. Combine the seasoning ingredients in a small bowl.
4. Combine the sauce ingredients in a small bowl.
5. Assemble your cooking tray.

Cooking

1. Grill or broil the steaks to desired doneness.
2. Heat a nonstick wok over high heat for 2 minutes.
3. Carefully spray the wok with the canola oil spray. (If you have a gas stove, turn off the burner before you spray the wok.) Add the seasonings and stir-fry for 30 seconds.
4. Add the sauce and stir about 30 seconds.
5. Arrange the steaks on a serving platter and place the blanched greens decoratively around the edge. Top with the heated sauce and garnish with the chives.

Each serving provides:
402 Calories
18 g Fat
7 g Saturated Fat
132 mg Cholesterol
9 g Carbohydrate
48 g Protein
370 mg Sodium

FRAGRANT SPICED BEEF ROAST

Makes 6 to 8 servings

Serve this as an entrée, then use the leftovers in our Fragrant Beef Buns (see index).

Marinade

2 cups low-sodium beef broth

1 small onion, coarsely chopped

3 slices fresh ginger, peeled and each about the size of a quarter

2 tablespoons dry sherry

2 tablespoons low-sodium soy sauce

2 tablespoons Chinese barbecue sauce (see note)

1 teaspoon minced fresh garlic

1 teaspoon five-spice powder

Meat

1 bottom round beef roast (2 1/2 to 3 pounds)

1. Preheat the oven to 350°.
2. Combine the marinade ingredients in a large heatproof casserole.
3. Place the roast in the casserole and cover.
4. Roast for 3 hours. Turn the roast over halfway through the cooking time.
5. Remove the casserole from the oven. Allow it to cool, then refrigerate overnight, covered.
6. The next day, remove the hardened layer of fat that has formed over the meat and sauce. Remove the meat and slice it thinly across the grain.
7. Bring the marinade to a boil and cook until it is reduced to 1 1/2 cups.

■

Each serving provides:

311 Calories

12 g Fat

4 g Saturated Fat

112 mg Cholesterol

4 g Carbohydrate

43 g Protein

203 mg Sodium

■

---

8. Serve the meat at room temperature. Place the sliced meat on a platter accompanied with the heated sauce in a separate bowl.

NOTE The flavor of Chinese barbecue sauce (also called Char Siu sauce) differs from western barbecue sauce. Seasoned with Chinese herbs and spices, it is made from soy beans, unlike the western tomato-based sauces. You can find Chinese barbecue sauce in the Asian foods section of most large supermarkets, or substitute hoisin sauce.

Mongolian Lamb and Scallions

Makes 3 to 4 servings

Although lamb is not often used in Chinese cooking, it is popular in the north of China and in Mongolia. In this dish, hoisin sauce adds a wonderful complementary flavor to the lamb.

Marinade
1 egg white, lightly beaten
1 tablespoon sesame oil
1 tablespoon low-sodium soy sauce
2 teaspoons cornstarch
1/2 teaspoon freshly ground black pepper

On Your Tray
- Canola oil spray
- Bowl of marinated lamb
- Bowl of seasonings
- Bowl of red pepper and scallions
- Bowl of sauce
- Cornstarch mixture

Meat
1 pound lean boneless leg of lamb, cut into 3/4-inch cubes

Seasonings
1 tablespoon minced fresh garlic
1 teaspoon minced fresh ginger

Vegetables
1/2 medium red bell pepper, seeds and ribs removed, coarsely chopped
8 scallions, both white and green parts, cut into 2-inch lengths

Sauce
1/2 cup low-sodium beef or chicken broth
1/4 cup dry white wine
2 tablespoons hoisin sauce
1 tablespoon low-sodium soy sauce

Additional Ingredients
1 tablespoon cornstarch dissolved in 2 tablespoons cold water
Canola oil spray

Preparation

1. Combine the marinade ingredients in a bowl and mix well to dissolve the cornstarch.
2. Add the lamb to the marinade and set aside for 20 to 30 minutes.
3. Combine the seasoning ingredients in a bowl.
4. Combine the red pepper and scallions in a small bowl.
5. Combine the sauce ingredients in another small bowl.
6. Assemble your cooking tray.

Cooking

1. Heat a nonstick wok over high heat for 2 minutes.
2. Carefully spray the wok with the canola oil spray. (If you have a gas stove, turn off the burner before you spray the wok.) Add the lamb and stir-fry for 2 minutes. Remove the lamb from the wok and set aside in a bowl.
3. Rinse out the wok, then reheat it for 30 seconds. Respray the wok with canola oil spray. Add the seasonings and stir-fry for 15 seconds.
4. Add the red pepper and scallions and stir-fry for 30 seconds.
5. Return the lamb to the wok and stir to heat through.
6. Stir in the sauce and bring to a boil. Add the cornstarch mixture and stir until thickened, about 30 seconds.
7. Remove from the wok and serve.

■

Each serving provides:
310 Calories
12 g Fat
4 g Saturated Fat
101 mg Cholesterol
11 g Carbohydrate
38 g Protein
337 mg Sodium

■

SZECHUAN LAMB WITH EGGPLANT AND SPINACH

Makes 3 to 4 servings

Using both chili pepper and chili paste, this dish is a bit hot, but the eggplant and spinach moderate the heat. As with all Szechuan recipes, you can make this more or less hot by adjusting the amount of chili peppers.

1 tablespoon low-sodium soy sauce

1 tablespoon dry sherry

8 ounces lean boneless leg of lamb, cut into 3/4-inch cubes

1 medium eggplant, peeled and cut into 3/4-inch cubes

1 teaspoon salt

10 ounces fresh spinach, washed and tough stems removed

ON YOUR TRAY

- Canola oil spray
- Bowl of marinated lamb
- Bowl of seasonings
- Bowl of eggplant
- Bowl of spinach
- Bowl of sauce

Seasonings

1/4 cup finely chopped onion

3 scallions, both white and green parts, finely chopped

2 teaspoons minced fresh green chili pepper

1 teaspoon minced fresh ginger

1 teaspoon minced fresh garlic

Sauce

2 tablespoons rice vinegar

1 tablespoon hoisin sauce

1 tablespoon low-sodium soy sauce

2 teaspoons chili paste

Additional Ingredient

Canola oil spray

Preparation

1. Combine the soy sauce and sherry in a bowl.
2. Add the lamb to the bowl and let marinate for 20 to 30 minutes.
3. Toss the eggplant with the salt and set aside in a colander for 30 minutes.
4. Rinse the eggplant in cold water, drain well, and place in a bowl. Place the spinach in another bowl.
5. Combine the seasoning ingredients in a small bowl.
6. Combine the sauce ingredients in another small bowl.
7. Assemble your cooking tray.

Cooking

1. Heat a nonstick wok over high heat for 2 minutes.
2. Carefully spray the wok with the canola oil spray. (If you have a gas stove, turn off the burner before you spray the wok.) Add the lamb and stir-fry for 2 minutes. Remove the lamb from the wok and set aside in a bowl.
3. Rinse out the wok, then reheat it for 30 seconds. Respray the wok with canola oil spray. Add the seasonings and stir-fry for 15 seconds.
4. Add the eggplant and stir-fry for 2 minutes.
5. Stir in the spinach, then cover, reduce the heat to low and simmer for 3 minutes.
6. Remove the cover, return the heat to high, and return the lamb to the wok.
7. Add the sauce and stir for 1 minute, or until heated through.
8. Remove from the wok and serve.

■

Each serving provides:
169 Calories
5 g Fat
2 g Saturated Fat
56 mg Cholesterol
9 g Carbohydrate
23 g Protein
422 mg Sodium

■

■ CURRIED YUNNAN LAMB

Makes 4 to 6 servings

Lamb and curries are part of the regional cuisine of Yunnan, a mountainous province in western China.

2 tablespoons low-sodium soy sauce
1 tablespoon dry sherry
1 tablespoon minced fresh garlic
1 pound lean boneless leg of lamb, trimmed of fat and cut into 3/4-inch cubes

ON YOUR TRAY

- Canola oil spray
- Bowl of marinated lamb
- Minced garlic
- Bowl of onions
- Bowl of sauce
- Bowl of cooked carrots
- Bowl of snow peas
- Cornstarch mixture

Vegetables

2 medium carrots, peeled and cut into 3/4-inch cubes
2 medium onions, peeled and each cut into 8 wedges
1 cup fresh snow peas (about 3 ounces), stems and strings removed

Sauce

1 1/2 cups low-sodium chicken broth
1 tablespoon curry powder
1 teaspoon Chinese hot oil

Additional Ingredients

1 tablespoon minced fresh garlic
1 1/2 tablespoons cornstarch dissolved in 3 tablespoons cold water
1 tablespoon chopped fresh coriander leaves for garnish
Canola oil spray

Preparation

1. Combine the soy sauce, sherry, and 1 tablespoon minced garlic in a bowl.
2. Add the lamb to the bowl and cover. Allow the lamb to marinate in the refrigerator for 3 hours, or overnight, turning the meat occasionally.
3. Bring water to a boil in a saucepan and cook the carrots for 3 to 4 minutes, or until tender. Drain and rinse them in cold water.
4. Place the carrots, onions, and snow peas in separate bowls.
5. Combine the sauce ingredients in a bowl.
6. Assemble your cooking tray.

Cooking

1. Heat a nonstick wok over high heat for 2 minutes.
2. Carefully spray the wok with the canola oil spray. (If you have a gas stove, turn off the burner before you spray the wok.) Add the lamb and stir-fry for 2 minutes. Remove the lamb from the wok and set aside.
3. Rinse out the wok, then reheat it for 30 seconds. Respray the wok with canola oil spray. Add the 1 tablespoon garlic and stir-fry for 10 seconds.
4. Add the onions and stir-fry for 2 minutes.
5. Stir in the sauce, cover, reduce the heat to medium, and cook for 3 minutes.
6. Remove the cover, add the carrots and snow peas and cook for 1 minute.
7. Return the lamb to the wok and stir to heat through.
8. Add the cornstarch mixture and stir until thickened, about 1 minute.
9. Remove from the wok and garnish with the coriander.

■

Each serving provides:
163 Calories
6 g Fat
2 g Saturated Fat
66 mg Cholesterol
9 g Carbohydrate
28 g Protein
192 mg Sodium

■

■ Hunan Lamb

Makes 3 to 4 servings

Many recipes from Hunan province, like those from Szechuan, use hot peppers to add spice. This lamb dish is a good example.

1 tablespoon low-sodium soy sauce
1 tablespoon dry sherry
1 tablespoon rice vinegar
8 ounces lean boneless leg of lamb, trimmed of fat and cut into thin strips 1/8 inch wide × 1 1/2 inches long

Seasonings

3 to 4 dried red chili peppers, each 1 1/2 to 2 inches long
1/2 cup finely chopped onion
1 tablespoon minced fresh ginger
1 tablespoon minced fresh garlic

On Your Tray

- Canola oil spray
- Bowl of marinated lamb
- Bowl of seasonings
- Bowl of broccoli
- Bowl of red pepper
- Bowl of sauce
- Cornstarch mixture

Vegetables

1 1/2 cups broccoli florets
2 medium red bell peppers, seeds and ribs removed, cut into 1-inch squares

Sauce

1 cup low-sodium chicken broth
2 tablespoons low-sodium soy sauce
1 teaspoon Chinese hot oil

Additional Ingredients

1 tablespoon cornstarch dissolved in 2 tablespoons cold water
Canola oil spray

Preparation

1. Combine 1 tablespoon soy sauce with the sherry and rice vinegar in a bowl.
2. Add the lamb to the bowl and let marinate for 20 to 30 minutes.
3. Combine the seasoning ingredients in a small bowl.
4. Place the broccoli and red pepper in separate bowls.
5. Combine the sauce ingredients in a small bowl.
6. Assemble your cooking tray.

Cooking

1. Heat a nonstick wok over high heat for 2 minutes.
2. Carefully spray the wok with the canola oil spray. (If you have a gas stove, turn off the burner before you spray the wok.) Add the lamb and stir-fry for 1 minute. Remove from the wok and set aside.
3. Rinse out the wok, then reheat it for 30 seconds. Respray the wok with canola oil spray. Add the seasonings and stir-fry for 30 seconds.
4. Add the broccoli and stir-fry for 1 minute.
5. Add the red pepper and stir-fry for 30 seconds.
6. Stir in the sauce, cover, and reduce the heat to medium. Cook for 3 minutes.
7. Remove the cover and return the lamb to the wok. Stir.
8. Add the cornstarch mixture, return the heat to high, and stir until the sauce is thickened, about 30 seconds.
9. Transfer to a serving platter. Remove and discard the chili peppers before serving.

Each serving provides:
146 Calories
5 g Fat
2 g Saturated Fat
57 mg Cholesterol
11 g Carbohydrate
18 g Protein
346 mg Sodium

ELEVEN

SAUCES AND GARNISHES

SPICY PEANUT SAUCE

SPICY SOY DIPPING SAUCE

SWEET DUCK SAUCE

CHINESE MUSTARD SAUCE

RADISH FLOWERS

SCALLION BRUSHES

■ SPICY PEANUT SAUCE

Makes 3/4 cup

    2 tablespoons low-sodium soy sauce
    1 tablespoon rice vinegar
    3 tablespoons fat-reduced peanut butter
    1 tablespoon honey
1/2 teaspoon minced fresh ginger
1/2 teaspoon minced fresh garlic
    3 tablespoons water
    1 teaspoon Chinese hot oil

1. Combine all the ingredients in a small bowl and mix until smooth and creamy.
2. Cover and refrigerate until ready to serve.

■

Each tablespoon provides:
51 Calories
3 g Fat
0.5 g Saturated Fat
0 mg Cholesterol
4 g Carbohydrate
2 g Protein
126 mg Sodium

■

SPICY SOY DIPPING SAUCE

Makes about ¹/₂ cup, serving 8

Serve this sauce with steamed dumplings and buns.

  2 tablespoons low-sodium soy sauce
  2 tablespoons water
  3 tablespoons rice vinegar
  1 teaspoon sugar
¹/₂ teaspoon sesame oil
¹/₂ teaspoon Chinese hot oil

1. Combine all the ingredients in a small bowl.
2. Cover and refrigerate until ready to serve.

Each serving provides:
8 Calories
0.5 g Fat
0.1 g Saturated Fat
0 mg Cholesterol
1 g Carbohydrate
0 g Protein
98 mg Sodium

■ Sweet Duck Sauce

Makes about 1 to 1¹/₄ cups, serving 16

Duck sauce is a popular Chinese sweet dipping sauce served with various appetizers and meat dishes. You can probably find duck sauce (also called plum sauce) in your supermarket, but here is a version you can make yourself.

¹/₂ cup mango chutney, coarsely chopped
¹/₂ cup apricot preserves
¹/₄ cup applesauce
 2 teaspoons water

1. Combine all the ingredients in a small bowl.
2. Cover and refrigerate until ready to serve.

■

Each serving provides:
42 Calories
0 g Fat
0 g Saturated Fat
0 mg Cholesterol
11 g Carbohydrate
0 g Protein
42 mg Sodium

■

■ CHINESE MUSTARD SAUCE

Makes about ½ cup, serving 12

Chinese mustard sauces are very hot. This is no exception, so use it sparingly.

2 tablespoons Chinese dry mustard powder
2 tablespoons water
1 teaspoon rice vinegar
1 teaspoon sugar

1. Combine all the ingredients in a small bowl.
2. Cover and refrigerate until ready to serve.

■

Each serving provides:
2 Calories
0 g Fat
0 g Saturated Fat
0 mg Cholesterol
1 g Carbohydrate
0 g Protein
40 mg Sodium

■

■ RADISH FLOWERS

Makes 12 roses

12 nicely shaped red radishes of similar size

1. Trim the root and stem ends of the radishes.
2. Using a very sharp paring knife, make several tiny cross-cuts, about 1/4-inch deep, in the stem end of each radish.
3. Place the radishes in a bowl of ice water for 1 hour, or overnight. The cut end of each radish will separate and open like the petals of a flower.
4. Store refrigerated in water until ready to use.

262

■ SCALLION BRUSHES

Makes 8 brushes

These brushes are both decorative and useful. The Chinese use them to brush hoisin sauce on the pancakes that are served with Mu shu dishes or Peking Duck.

8 scallions

1. Trim the root ends of the scallions.
2. Cut off the green end of the scallion and save for another recipe.
3. Using a very sharp paring knife, make several cross-cuts 1 inch deep in each root end.
4. Put the scallions in a bowl of ice water for 1 hour, or overnight. The cut ends will separate and curl to resemble paint brushes.
5. Store refrigerated in water until ready to use.

TWELVE

DESSERTS AND TEA

GRILLED PINEAPPLE WITH GINGER GLAZE

STEAMED APPLES AND PEARS WITH TOASTED ALMONDS

STARDUST FRUIT

ORANGE RICE PUDDING

MANGO SORBET

TRIPLE CITRUS SORBET

CHINESE TEA

GRILLED PINEAPPLE WITH GINGER GLAZE

Makes 6 to 8 servings

This tasty pineapple concoction may be served as a dessert or as an accompaniment to a pork, chicken, or turkey entrée.

3 tablespoons brown sugar

2 teaspoons minced fresh ginger

1 fresh pineapple, peeled, cored, and sliced

1 cup orange juice

1 pint fresh strawberries, rinsed and stems removed, for garnish

1. Combine the brown sugar and ginger and set aside.
2. Preheat the oven to 400°.
3. Arrange the pineapple in a heatproof 9 × 13-inch baking dish.
4. Pour the orange juice over the pineapple and sprinkle the top with the brown sugar mixture.
5. Bake 5 minutes to heat through, then place under the broiler until lightly browned, about 3 minutes.
6. Serve on individual plates garnished with 2 or 3 strawberries.

Each serving provides:
102 Calories
0.8 g Fat
0.1 g Saturated Fat
0 mg Cholesterol
25 g Carbohydrate
1 g Protein
4 mg Sodium

STEAMED APPLES AND PEARS WITH TOASTED ALMONDS

Makes 6 servings

2 large ripe pears, peeled, cored, and cut into 8 wedges
2 large ripe apples, peeled, cored, and cut into 8 wedges
1/4 cup raisins
3 tablespoons frozen apple juice concentrate
1 teaspoon lemon juice
1/4 teaspoon ground cinnamon
   Zest of 1 lemon
1/4 cup sliced almonds, lightly browned in a dry skillet
    over medium heat

1. Bring 3 to 4 inches of water to a boil in a wok.
2. Arrange the pear and apple wedges in a heatproof bowl that fits in the rack of a bamboo steamer. Sprinkle the raisins over the top.
3. Combine the apple juice and lemon juice and pour over the fruit.
4. Lightly sprinkle the top with the cinnamon.
5. Cover the steamer and place it in the wok over the boiling water and steam for 8 minutes.
6. When cool enough to handle, remove the bowl from the steamer and sprinkle the fruit with the lemon zest.
7. Serve warm or cold, sprinkled with the toasted almonds.

> ■
> Each serving provides:
> 127 Calories
> 3 g Fat
> 0.3 g Saturated Fat
> 0 mg Cholesterol
> 25 g Carbohydrate
> 2 g Protein
> 3 mg Sodium
> ■

■ STARDUST FRUIT

Makes 6 servings

When a bowl of just plain fruit is not enough to satisfy your taste buds, this sesame-caramel "stardust" comes to the rescue.

Stardust

    Canola oil spray

1 cup granulated white sugar

2 teaspoons sesame seeds, lightly browned in a dry skillet over medium heat

Fruit

2 large bananas, peeled and sliced

1 can (11 ounces) mandarin oranges in light syrup, drained

1/2 small melon, peeled and cut into 1-inch cubes

1 cup orange juice

1. Spray a baking sheet with canola oil spray.
2. Put the sugar in a heavy stainless steel saucepan over medium heat, stirring occasionally with a wooden spoon. The sugar will melt and start to turn a golden color.
3. When the sugar has turned the color of iced tea, remove the pan from the heat and pour the hot sugar syrup onto the baking sheet. Sprinkle the top of the caramelized syrup with the sesame seeds.
4. When the caramel has cooled and become brittle, break it into pieces. Put the pieces into a food processor or blender to process to a coarse powder. The stardust can be stored up to 3 months in an airtight container.
5. Combine the fruit in a serving bowl.
6. Pour the orange juice over the fruit and refrigerate until ready to serve.
7. When ready to serve, divide the fruit among individual serving bowls and sprinkle each serving with 1 teaspoon of the stardust.

■

Each serving provides:
184 Calories
1 g Fat
0.2 g Saturated Fat
0 mg Cholesterol
44 g Carbohydrate
2 g Protein
14 mg Sodium

■

■ Orange Rice Pudding

Makes 6 servings

  1 can (12 ounces) evaporated skim milk
 1/2 cup orange juice
  3 tablespoons cornstarch
 1/4 cup sugar
 1/2 cup Chinese-Style Boiled Rice (see index)
 1/2 teaspoon orange extract
  1 tablespoon orange zest

1. Combine the evaporated milk and the orange juice in a pitcher.
2. Combine the cornstarch and sugar in a saucepan and mix well off the heat.
3. Place the saucepan over medium-high heat.
4. Slowly pour in the evaporated milk mixture, stirring continuously with a whisk to avoid lumps.
5. Bring to a boil, add the rice, and stir to combine.
6. Reduce the heat to medium-low and simmer for 5 or 6 minutes, stirring continuously.
7. Remove the saucepan from the heat and stir in the orange extract and orange zest.
8. Pour the pudding into a serving bowl, cover with plastic wrap, and refrigerate for several hours before serving.

■

Each serving provides:
182 Calories
0.2 g Fat
0.1 g Saturated Fat
2 mg Cholesterol
38 g Carbohydrate
6 g Protein
76 mg Sodium

■

◼ MANGO SORBET

Makes about 1 quart, serving 4 to 6

This recipe works best if you have an ice-cream maker. We use a simple manual version made by Donvier. It is inexpensive and easy to use, but any machine will do just as well.

1/2 cup sugar
1/2 cup water
  4 ripe mangoes, peeled and pitted
  2 tablespoons fresh lemon juice
  1 tablespoon lemon zest

1. Combine the sugar and water in a small saucepan and bring to a boil. Cook 2 to 3 minutes, until the sugar is dissolved. Set aside to cool.
2. Purée the mango in a food processor or blender.
3. Stir the mango purée into the sugar syrup and refrigerate to chill, about 30 minutes.
4. Stir in the lemon juice and lemon zest.
5. Pour the mixture into an ice-cream maker and freeze according to the manufacturer's directions. Don't make a sorbet too far in advance—it tastes better when it has been freshly made.

◼

Each serving provides:
155 Calories
0.4 g Fat
0.1 g Saturated Fat
0 mg Cholesterol
40 g Carbohydrate
1 g Protein
6 mg Sodium

◼

DESSERTS AND TEA

■ TRIPLE CITRUS SORBET

Makes about 1 quart, serving 4 to 6

   1 cup sugar
   1/4 cup fresh lime juice
   1/4 cup fresh lemon juice
   3 cups orange juice
   1 teaspoon finely chopped lemon zest
   1 teaspoon finely chopped lime zest
   1 teaspoon finely chopped orange zest

1. Combine the sugar, lime juice, and lemon juice
   in a small saucepan and bring to a boil. Cook 1 to
   2 minutes, until the sugar is dissolved.
2. Remove pan from the heat and stir in the orange
   juice. Refrigerate to chill, about 30 minutes.
3. Stir in the fruit zests.
4. Pour the mixture into an ice-cream maker and
   freeze according to the manufacturer's directions.

■

Each serving provides:
189 Calories
0.3 g Fat
0.1 g Saturated Fat
0 mg Cholesterol
47 g Carbohydrate
1 g Protein
5 mg Sodium

■

DESSERTS AND TEA

Chinese Tea

Makes 6 servings

Tea is the beverage of choice for most Chinese people. Several kinds of Chinese tea are available. Green tea, made from the best leaves of the plant, is the lightest, most delicate, and usually most prized of the Chinese teas. Black tea—the tea usually served in Chinese restaurants—is made from slightly fermented tea leaves and has a stronger flavor and aroma than green tea. Oolong tea, which is also fermented, is somewhat blander than black tea. Aromatic teas, such as Jasmine tea, have flower or fruit blossoms mixed in. Try the different kinds of Chinese teas and use the one you prefer. The best selections of teas can be found in Asian markets, but health food stores and supermarkets also carry some.

The Chinese care a great deal about the quality of tea and how to brew it to bring out its special flavor. Here is our way of preparing Chinese tea.

6 cups water
3 teaspoons loose tea

1. Warm your teapot by filling it first with boiling water. Set aside for 2 or 3 minutes and then empty it. This will help to keep the tea hot longer.
2. Bring the water for the tea to a rapid boil in a saucepan.
3. Spoon the tea leaves into the warmed teapot.
4. Pour 1 inch of boiling water over the tea leaves and allow it to steep for 3 minutes.
5. Add the remainder of the boiling water and serve.

■

Each serving provides:
0 Calories
0 g Fat
0 g Saturated Fat
0 mg Cholesterol
0 g Carbohydrate
0 g Protein
5 mg Sodium

■

DESSERTS AND TEA

CHINESE INGREDIENTS

Most of the ingredients used in this book are the same vegetables, meats, seafood, herbs, and spices you use regularly in all your cooking.

Listed here are some special Chinese sauces, vegetables, and spices that may or may not be familiar to you.

baby corn   These miniature ears of corn are a colorful part of some stir-fry recipes. You can buy them in cans in Asian markets and at most supermarkets.

bean sprouts   These edible sprouts are generally grown from either soy beans or mung beans. Mung bean sprouts are used more often because of their delicate flavor. Fresh sprouts are preferred over the canned version.

black bean sauce   This distinctively flavored sauce made from fermented, highly salted beans, is much favored by the Chinese. It is sometimes combined with garlic. Black bean sauce is available in Asian markets and in some well-stocked supermarkets.

bok choy/Chinese cabbage   This delicious vegetable is readily available in most supermarkets and produce shops. Its milky white stalks and dark green leaves are highly nutritious.

cellophane noodles   These delicate, transparent noodles are made from mung beans rather than from flour and eggs. They are sometimes called bean threads or Chinese vermicelli and are popularly used in soups and stir-fry recipes. If you can't find them in your market, substitute thin spaghetti.

chili paste   This fiery combination of chili peppers, spices, and sometimes garlic is a common ingredient in Szechuan dishes. Fresh green chilies can be substituted.

chili peppers   Dried red chili peppers frequently are used in Szechuan and Hunan recipes and can be found in the produce section of most supermarkets. These dried peppers are very hot and are not intended to be eaten themselves. Used in cooking to give flavor to sauces, the peppers should be removed and discarded before the dish is served. If you like more or less spice, adjust the amount of peppers that the recipe calls for. You can make the peppers themselves less hot by snipping off the tip and shaking out and discarding some or most of the seeds—the hottest part of peppers—before you use them.

   Many of our recipes, particularly the spicy sauces, also call for fresh green chili peppers. They can be found in the produce section of your market.

Chinese dry mustard   This mustard is very hot, so use it carefully. You may prefer using a milder western-style mustard. Chinese dry mustard is available in Asian markets and some well-stocked supermarkets.

Chinese egg noodles   These are generally found now in the produce section of most markets. They are made from wheat flour and eggs and give the best results when cooking lo mein dishes. You can also use Japanese noodles or other fresh egg noodles. In a pinch, you can substitute regular dried pasta. Please note that some recipes may call for cellophane noodles or rice noodles. These have a difference taste and consistency. Please also refer to those definitions.

Chinese hot (chili) oil   This spicy hot seasoning is used in dipping sauces and some other recipes. It is generally made with sesame oil and dried red chilies. If unavailable, substitute Tabasco.

coriander (Chinese parsley)   This fresh herb is sometimes called cilantro. Coriander has a distinctive fresh herbal taste and we like it as a seasoning in Chinese foods. We don't use too much or it dominates a dish's other flavors. Coriander can be used like parsley as a garnish, but when it is used as a flavoring, we generally mince the leaves.

duck sauce   See plum sauce.

dumpling (or wonton) wrappers   These wrappers can be bought in Asian markets and some supermarkets. You can make your own, but even the Chinese rarely do that. Once purchased, the wrappers can be refrigerated for several days or, if wrapped well, stored in the freezer for up to several months. Dumpling and wonton wrappers are made from the same ingredients, but dumpling wrappers are round and wonton wrappers are square. If you can only find one or the other, you can make do with whichever you find.

five-spice powder This finely ground spice is a combination of cloves, fennel, cinnamon, anise, and ginger. If you can't find it, try using equal amounts of each spice to create your own.

garlic Garlic is an omnipresent Chinese flavoring. Fresh garlic is preferred, but you may wish to use store-bought minced garlic, which is sold in a jar.

ginger This pungent, flavored root is very popular in Asian cuisines, particularly Chinese. It can be bought fresh as a small, brown, knobby root, or, like garlic, it can now be purchased, minced, in a jar. To preserve fresh ginger in your refrigerator, peel it and store it in dry sherry in a covered container. Or you can freeze it, peeled, in recipe-sized pieces. When using fresh ginger in a recipe, peel off the brown outer skin and mince it, either with a knife or in your food processor. Some recipes will call for thin slices rather than minced ginger.

hoisin sauce This mildly spicy, very flavorful thick brown sauce is extremely popular in Chinese cuisine. Made from soy beans, various spices, and chilies, hoisin sauce is easily found in supermarkets.

mushrooms, dried Chinese These meaty-textured mushrooms are delicate in flavor and add a subtle, yet distinctive, taste to food. You can substitute the Japanese equivalent, shiitake mushrooms, which are found in most supermarkets. Dried mushrooms should be rinsed before using and softened in hot water for about 30 minutes. The tough stems should be removed and discarded before proceeding with the recipe.

oyster sauce This sauce is indeed made from oysters, along with various vegetable ingredients. It is a frequently used flavoring, particularly in Cantonese dishes, and has a pungent taste. You can buy it bottled in most supermarkets. Once opened, the bottle should be kept in the refrigerator.

pine nuts These light beige nuts are softer and smaller than peanuts and more subtle in flavor. They add crunch to various Chinese recipes.

plum sauce This thick, fruit-based sauce is similar to a chutney. Sometimes called duck sauce, it is used as a condiment for various dim sum and meats.

rice noodles   These noodles, sometimes called rice sticks, are made from rice flour rather than wheat flour. Substitute vermicelli if you can't find rice noodles.

rice vinegar   This Asian variety of vinegar is less astringent than American cider vinegars. It gives a pleasing tang to a recipe, more like lemon juice than vinegar.

rice wine   Another flavoring agent in Chinese sauces, it is often used in marinades for meats or seafood. You can buy Chinese rice wine for this purpose, or use a dry cocktail sherry, as we do in the recipes in this book.

sesame oil   Chinese sesame oil is pressed from toasted sesame seeds and is darker in color and richer in flavor than other sesame oils on the market. It is high in calories, so we use it sparingly in our recipes in this book. Chinese sesame oil is available in most markets. A Japanese brand of toasted sesame oil may be substituted.

sesame paste   This paste is made from toasted sesame seeds and soy beans. Like sesame oil, it has a nutty aroma and taste. Sesame paste is high in fat, so we don't use it often. Sesame paste should be refrigerated once the jar is opened.

soy sauce   Made from soy beans, soy sauce is one of the most frequently used Chinese seasonings. It is very low in calories, but, unfortunately, is very high in sodium. Definitely buy a low-sodium version. Even so, most low-sodium brands are far from being really low in sodium. In our versions of traditional recipes, we cut back on the amount of soy sauce used, and in some cases have cut it out entirely.

spring roll wrappers   These wrappers are thinner and more delicate than traditional egg roll wrappers. You can find them, refrigerated, in Asian markets and at some well-stocked supermarkets. They can be stored, well wrapped, in your freezer.

star anise   This spice looks like a multi-pointed star and tastes like licorice. We rarely use it in our recipes, so if you can't find star anise, substitute the powdered version found in supermarkets.

straw mushrooms   These small, lightly colored cone-shaped mushrooms have a delicate taste and texture. You can find them most commonly in cans, but they also are available dried. If using dried straw mushrooms, rinse them first in cold water, then soak them in hot water for 30 minutes to soften before proceeding with the recipe.

water chestnuts   This popular vegetable adds a contrasting texture and crunch to many Chinese dishes. Water chestnuts can be bought fresh at Asian markets, but the canned variety is easier to find. Once the can is opened, store the remaining water chestnuts in fresh water in a closed plastic container in the refrigerator. If you change the water every two or three days, they will keep for a couple of weeks. If you do find fresh water chestnuts in your market, definitely give them a try. They have a more distinctive, sweeter taste than the canned version. With fresh water chestnuts, wash them well, peel off the outer skin, and slice them thinly before adding to a recipe.

INDEX

More Cookbooks from Prima Publishing

The Best of Vietnamese and Thai Cooking: Favorite Recipes from Lemon Grass Restaurant and Cafes

by Mai Pham
$18.95

Learn to cook the food that has made the Lemon Grass Restaurant and Cafes famous! Well-loved restaurateur Mai Pham discloses the secrets to her hallmark dipping sauces, soups, noodles, stir-fry dishes, and more. Hand-picked recipes from the restaurant mingle with stories from the author's childhood to create a magical formula for mouth-watering dishes. A beautiful new favorite for your cookbook collection.

The Good-for-You Garlic Cookbook: Over 125 Deliciously Healthful Garlic Recipes

by Linda Ferrari
$12.95

Here's proof that the best things in life don't have to be bad for you. Now you can reap all the health benefits of the delicious garlic bulb and leave behind its traditional companions, fat and sodium. Feast on savory, healthful dishes such as potato garlic soup, chicken pasta with plum wine, lamb with pears and mint, garlicky pasta and crab salad, light paella, and more! Each recipe includes a complete nutritional breakdown.

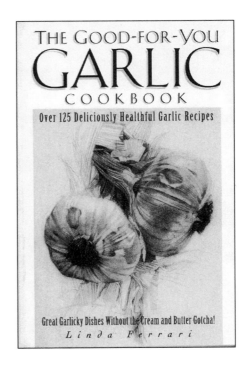

Hot & Spicy Southeast Asian Dishes: The Best Fiery Food from the Pacific Rim

by Dave DeWitt, Mary Jane Wilan, and Melissa T. Stock
$14.95

You'll love this sizzling new collection from the editors of *Chile Pepper Magazine*. Share in the authors' culinary adventures as they trek across the backroads of Thailand, Singapore, and Malaysia. Visit a riverside chile vendor in Bangkok. Learn the fascinating history of chiles and spices. The great chile pepper love affair continues with the succulent curries, soups, and stir-fry dishes of the Pacific Rim!

The Lowfat Grill: 175 Surprisingly Succulent Recipes for Meats, Marinades, Vegetables, Sauces, and More!

by Donna Rodnitzky
$16.95

Though what's usually put to the flame is sinfully fattening, it doesn't have to be! *The Lowfat Grill* shows you how to choose leaner cuts of meat, exchange heavy sauces for light and savory complements, and use professional techniques to enjoy that distinctive smoky flavor in a lean and healthful way. From steaks and kebabs to seafood, poultry, and fruit, here are recipes to transform all your favorite ingredients into tender, delicious grilled specialties. Each recipe includes a complete nutritional breakdown.

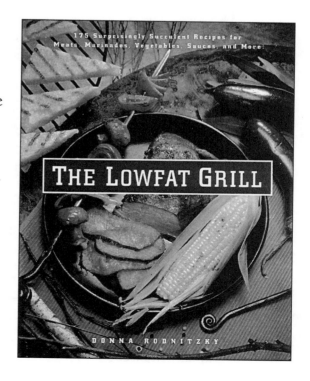

I'd like to order copies of the following titles:

Quantity	Title	Amount
_____	*The Best of Vietnamese and Thai Cooking: Favorite Recipes from Lemon Grass Restaurant and Cafes* $18.95	_____
_____	*The Good-for-You Garlic Cookbook: Over 125 Deliciously Healthful Garlic Recipes* $12.95	_____
_____	*Hot & Spicy Southeast Asian Dishes: The Best Fiery Food from the Pacific Rim* $14.95	_____
_____	*The Lowfat Grill: 175 Surprisingly Succulent Recipes for Meats, Marinades, Vegetables, Sauces, and More!* $16.95	_____
	Subtotal	_____
	Postage & Handling ($3 for first book, $1 for additional books)	_____
	7.25% Sales Tax (California only)	_____
	TOTAL (U.S. funds only)	_____

Check enclosed for $_____ (payable to Prima Publishing)

Charge my ☐ MasterCard ☐ Visa

Account No. _____ Exp. Date _____

Signature _____

Your Name _____

Address _____

City/State/Zip _____

Daytime Telephone (___) _____